The Meaning of Good

A Dialogue

I0887701

G. Lowes Dickinson

Routledge Revivals

Routledge
Taylor & Francis Group

First published in 1937
by George Allen & Unwin LTD

This edition first published in 2016 by Routledge
2 Park Square, Milton Park, Abingdon, Oxon, OX14 4RN
and by Routledge
711 Third Avenue, New York, NY 10017

Routledge is an imprint of the Taylor & Francis Group, an informa business

Publisher's Note
The publisher has gone to great lengths to ensure the quality of this reprint but points out that some imperfections in the original copies may be apparent.

Disclaimer
The publisher has made every effort to trace copyright holders and welcomes correspondence from those they have been unable to contact.

ISBN 13: 978-1-138-95788-6 (hbk)
ISBN 13: 978-1-315-66147-6 (ebk)
ISBN 13: 978-1-138-95789-3 (pbk)

Routledge Revivals

The Meaning of Good

First published in 1937, this book presents itself as a philosophic dialogue, starting with the diversity of men's ideas about Good. In the first part, it considers the creation and criteria of Good and its relation to truth, pleasure and happiness. In the second part, the book examines some kinds of Good, pointing out their defects and limitations, and suggesting the character of Good which we might hold to be perfect. The topic of the book is treated both philosophically and practically making it intriguing reading.

THE MEANING OF GOOD · A DIALOGUE

by

G. LOWES DICKINSON

LONDON
GEORGE ALLEN & UNWIN LTD
MUSEUM STREET

SEVENTH IMPRESSION 1937

DEDICATION

How do the waves along the level shore
  Follow and fly in hurrying sheets of foam,
For ever doing what they did before,
  For ever climbing what is never clomb!
Is there an end to their perpetual haste,
  Their iterated round of low and high,
Or is it one monotony of waste
  Under the vision of the vacant sky?
And thou, who on the ocean of thy days
  Dost like a swimmer patiently contend,
And though thou steerest with a shoreward gaze
  Misdoubtest of a harbour or an end,
What would the threat, or what the promise be,
  Could I but read the riddle of the sea!

PRINTED IN GREAT BRITAIN BY
UNWIN BROTHERS LIMITED, LONDON AND WOKING

PREFACE

An attempt at Philosophic Dialogue may seem to demand a word of explanation, if not of apology. For, it may be said, the Dialogue is a literary form not only exceedingly difficult to handle, but, in its application to philosophy, discredited by a long series of failures. I am not indifferent to this warning; yet I cannot but think that I have chosen the form best suited to my purpose. For, in the first place, the problems I have undertaken to discuss have an interest not only philosophic but practical; and I was ambitious to treat them in a way which might perhaps appeal to some readers who are not professed students of philosophy. And, secondly, my subject is one which belongs to the sphere of right opinion and perception, rather than to that of logic and demonstration; and seems therefore to be properly approached in the tentative spirit favoured by the Dialogue form. On such topics most men, I think, will feel that it is in conversation that they get their best lights; and Dialogue is merely an attempt to reproduce in literary form this natural genesis of opinion. Lastly, my own attitude in approaching the issues with which I have dealt was, I found, so little dogmatic, so sincerely speculative, that I should have felt myself hampered by the form of a treatise. I was more desirous to set forth various points of view than finally to repudiate or endorse them ; and though I have taken occasion to suggest certain opinions of my own, I have endeavoured to do so in the way which should be least imprisoning to my own thought, and least provocative of the reader's antagonism. It has been my object, to borrow a phrase of Renan, 'de présenter des séries d'idées se développant selon un ordre logique, et non d'inculquer une opinion ou de prêcher un systême déterminé.' And I may add, with him, 'Moins que jamais je me sens l'audace de parler doctrinalement en pareille matière.'

In conclusion, there is one defect which is, I think, inherent in the Dialogue form, even if it were treated with far greater skill than any to which I can pretend. The connection of the various phases of the discussion can hardly be as clearly marked as it would be in a formal treatise ; and in the midst of digressions and interruptions, such as are natural in conversation, the main thread of the reasoning may sometimes be lost. I have therefore appended a brief summary of the argument, set forth in its logical connections.

ARGUMENT

BOOK I.

PAGES

I. After a brief introduction, the discussion starts with a consideration of the diversity of men's ideas about Good, a diversity which suggests *primâ facie* a scepticism as to the truth of any of these ideas. 1-6

The sceptical position is stated; and, in answer, an attempt is made to show that the position is one which is not really accepted by thinking men. For such men, it is maintained, regulate their lives by their ideas about Good, and thus by implication admit their belief in these ideas. 6-19

This is admitted; but the further objection is made, that for the regulation of life it is only necessary for a man to admit a Good for himself, without admitting also a General Good or Good of all. It is suggested, in reply, that the conduct of thinking men commonly does imply a belief in a General Good. 19-26

Against this it is urged that the belief implied is not in a Good of all, but merely in the mutual compatibility of the Goods of individuals; so that each whilst pursuing exclusively his own Good,

PAGES

metaphysical, and *a priori*. In reply, the bare possibility of such a method is admitted; but it is urged that no one really believes that all our opinions derived from experience are false, and that such a belief, if held, would deprive life of all ethical significance and worth. 73-79

Finally, it is suggested that the position in which we do actually find ourselves, is that of men who have a real, though imperfect perception of a real Good, and who are endeavouring, by practice, to perfect that perception. In this respect an analogy is drawn between our perception of Good and our perception of Beauty.

It is further suggested that the end of life is not merely a knowledge but an experience of Good; this end being conceived as one to be realised in Time. 79-89

IV. On this, the point is raised, whether it is not necessary to conceive Good as eternally existing, rather than as something to be brought into existence in the course of Time? On this view, Evil must be conceived as mere 'appearance.'

In reply, it is suggested:

(1) That it is impossible to reconcile the conception of eternal Good with the obvious fact of temporal Evil.

(2) That such a view reduces to an absurdity all action directed to ends in Time. And yet it seems that such action not only is but ought to be pursued, as appears to be admitted even by those who hold that Good exists eternally, since they make it

PAGES

an end of action that they should come to see that everything is good.

(3) That this latter conception of the end of action—namely, that we should bring ourselves to see that what appears to be Evil is really Good—is too flagrantly opposed to common sense to be seriously accepted. 90-104

To sum up:

In this Book the following positions have been discussed and rejected:

(1) That our ideas about Good have no relation to any real fact.

(2) That we have easy and simple criteria of Good—such as (*a*) an infallible instinct, (*b*) the course of Nature, (*c*) current conventions, (*d*) pleasure.

(3) That all Reality is good, and all Evil is mere 'appearance.'

And it has been suggested that our experience is, or may be made, a progressive discovery of Good.

In the following Book the question of the content of Good is approached.

BOOK II.

This Book comprises an attempt to examine some kinds of Good, to point out their defects and limitations, and to suggest the character of a Good which we might hold to be perfect—here referred to as '*The* Good.'

PAGES

The attitude adopted is tentative, for it is based on the position, at which we are supposed to have arrived, that the experience of any one person, or set of persons, about Good is limited and imperfect, and that therefore in any attempt to describe what it is that we hold to be good, to compare Goods among one another, and to suggest an absolute Good, we can only hope, at best, to arrive at some approximation to truth.

I. This attitude is explained at the outset, and certain preliminary points are then discussed. These are: 105-108

(1) Can any Good be an end for us unless it is conceived to be an object of consciousness? The negative answer is suggested. 108-110

(2) In pursuing Good, for whom do we pursue it? It is suggested that the Good we pursue is

(*a*) That of future generations. Some difficulties in this view are brought out; and it is hinted that what we really pursue is the Good of 'the Whole,' though it is not easy to see what we mean by that. 110-119

(*b*) That of 'the species.' But this view too is seen to be involved in difficulty. 119-128

II. The difficulty is left unsolved, and the conversation passes on to an examination of some of our activities from the point of view of Good. In this examination a double object is kept in view: (1) to bring out the characteristics and defects of each kind of Good; (2) to suggest a Good which might be conceived to be free from defects, such a Good being referred to as '*The* Good.'

PAGES

On the other hand, the Good of Art suffers from the defects:

(*a*) That outside and independent of Art there is the 'real world,' so that this Good is only a partial one.

(*b*) That Art is a creation of man, whereas we seem to demand, for a thing that shall be perfectly good, that it shall be so of its own nature, without our intervention. 151-160

(5) It is suggested that perhaps we may find the Good we seek in knowledge. This raises the difficulty that various views are held as to the nature of knowledge. Of these, two are discussed:

(*a*) the view that knowledge is 'the description and summing up in brief formulae, of the routine of our perceptions.' It is questioned whether there is really much Good in such an activity. And it is argued that, whatever Good it may have, it cannot be *the* Good, seeing that knowledge may be, and frequently is, knowledge of Bad. 160-167

(*b*) the view that knowledge consists in the perception of 'necessary connections.' Viewed from the standpoint of Good, this seems to be open to the same objection as (*a*). But, further, it is argued that the perpetual contemplation of necessary relations among ideas does not satisfy our conception of the Good; but that we require an element analogous somehow to

PAGES

that of sense, though not, like sense, unintelligible and obscure. 167-172

(6) Finally, it is suggested that in our relation to other persons, where the relation takes the form of love, we may perhaps find something that comes nearer than any other of our experiences to being absolutely good. For in that relation, it is urged, we are in contact

(*a*) with objects, not 'mere ideas.'

(*b*) with objects that are good in themselves and

(*c*) intelligible and

(*d*) harmonious to our own nature.

It is objected that love, so conceived, is

(*a*) rarely, perhaps never, experienced.

(*b*) in any case, is neither eternal nor universal.

This is admitted; but it is maintained that the best love we know comes nearer than anything else to what we might conceive to be absolutely good. 172-187

III. The question is now raised: if 'the Good' be so conceived, is it not clearly unattainable? The answer to this question seems to depend on whether or not we believe in personal immortality. The following points are therefore discussed:

(*a*) Whether personal immortality is conceivable?

(*b*) Whether a belief in it is essential to a reasonable pursuit of Good? 187-209

On these points no dogmatic solution is offered; and the Dialogue closes with the description of a dream. 209-224

BOOK I.

Every summer, for several years past, it has been my custom to arrange in some pleasant place, either in England or on the continent, a gathering of old college friends. In this way I have been enabled not only to maintain some happy intimacies, but (what to a man of my occupation is not unimportant) to refresh and extend, by an interchange of ideas with men of various callings, an experience of life which might be otherwise unduly monotonous and confined. Last year, in particular, our meeting was rendered to me especially agreeable by the presence of a very dear friend, Philip Audubon, whom, since his business lay in the East, I had not had an opportunity of seeing for many years. I mention him particularly, because, although, as will be seen, he did not take much part in the discussion I am about to describe, he was, in a sense, the originator of it. For, in the first place, it was he who had invited us to the place in which we were staying,—an upland valley in Switzerland, where he had taken a house; and, further, it was through my renewed intercourse with him that I was led into the train of thought which issued in the following conversation. His life in the East, a life laborious and monotonous in the extreme, had confirmed in him a melancholy to which he was constitutionally inclined, and which appeared to be rather heightened than diminished by exceptional success in a difficult career. I hesitate to describe his attitude as pessimistic, for the word has associations with the schools from which he was singularly free. His melancholy was not the artificial product of a philosophic system ; it was temperamental rather than intellectual, and might be described, perhaps, as an intuition rather than a judgment of the worthlessness and irrationality of the world. Such a position is not readily shaken by argument, nor did I make any direct attempt to assail it ; but it could not fail to impress itself strongly upon my mind, and to keep my thoughts constantly employed upon that old problem of the worth of things, in which, indeed, for other reasons, I was already sufficiently interested.

A further impulse in the same direction was given by the arrival of another old friend, Arthur Ellis. He and I had been drawn together at college by a common interest in philosophy ; but in later years our paths had diverged widely. Fortune and inclination had led him into an active career, and for some years he had been travelling abroad as correspondent to one of the daily papers. I felt, therefore, some curiosity to renew my acquaintance with him, and to ascertain how far his views had been modified by his experience of the world.

The morning after his arrival he joined Audubon and myself in a kind of loggia at the back of the house, which was our common place of rendezvous. We exchanged the usual greetings, and for some minutes nothing more was said, so pleasant was it to sit silent in the shade listening to the swish of scythes (they were cutting the grass in the meadow opposite) and to the bubbling of a little fountain in the garden on our right, while the sun grew hotter every minute on the fir-covered slopes beyond. I wanted to talk, and yet I was unwilling to begin; but presently Ellis turned to me and said: "Well, my dear philosopher, and how goes the world with you? What have you been doing in all these years since we met?"

"Oh," I replied, "nothing worth talking about."

"What have you been thinking then?"

"Just now I have been thinking how well you look. Knocking about the world seems to suit you."

"I think it does. And yet at this moment, whether it be the quiet of the place, or whether it be the sight of your philosophic countenance, I feel a kind of yearning for the contemplative life. I believe if I stayed here long you would lure me back to philosophy; and yet I thought I had finally escaped when I broke away from you before."

"It is not so easy," I said, "to escape from that net, once one is caught. But it was not I who spread the snare; I was only trying to help you out, or, at least, to get out myself."

"And have you found a way?"

"No, I cannot say that I have. That's why I want to talk to you and hear how you have fared."

"I? Oh, I have given the whole subject up."

"You can hardly give up the subject till you give

up life. You may have given up reading books about it; and, for that matter, so have I. But that is only because I want to grapple with it more closely."

"What do you do, then, if you do not read books?"

"I talk to as many people as I can, and especially to those who have had no special education in philosophy; and try to find out to what conclusions they have been led by their own direct experience."

"Conclusions about what?"

"About many things. But in particular about the point we used to be fondest of discussing in the days before you had, as you say, given up the subject—I mean the whole question of the values we attach, or ought to attach, to things."

"Oh!" he said, "well, as to all that, my opinion is the same as of old. 'There's nothing good or bad but thinking makes it so.' So I used to say at college and so I say now."

"I remember," I replied, "that that is what you always used to say; but I thought I had refuted you over and over again."

"So you may have done, as far as logic can refute; but every bit of experience which I have had since last we met has confirmed me in my original view."

"That," I said, "is very interesting, and is just what I want to hear about. What is it that experience has done for you? For, as you know, I have so little of my own, I try to get all I can out of other people's."

"Well," he said, "the effect of mine has been to bring home to me, in a way I could never realize before, the extraordinary diversity of men's ideals."

"That, you find, is the effect of travel?"

"I think so. Travelling really does open the eyes. For instance, until I went to the East I never really felt the antagonism between the Oriental view of life and our own. Now, it seems to me clear that either they are mad or we are; and upon my word, I don't know which. Of course, when one is here, one supposes it is they. But when one gets among them and really talks to them, when one realizes how profound and intelligent is their contempt for our civilization, how worthless they hold our aims and activities, how illusory our progress, how futile our intelligence, one begins to wonder whether, after all, it is not merely by an effect of habit that one judges them to be wrong and ourselves right, and whether there is anything at all except blind prejudice in any opinions and ideas about Right and Wrong."

"In fact," interposed Audubon, "you agree, like me, with Sir Richard Burton:

There is no good, there is no bad, these be the whims of mortal will;
What works me weal that call I good, what harms and hurts I hold as ill.
They change with space, they shift with race, and in the veriest span of time,
Each vice has worn a virtue's crown, all good been banned as sin or crime."

"Yes," he assented, "and that is what is brought home to one by travel. Though really, if one had penetration enough, it would not be necessary to travel to make the discovery. A single country, a single city, almost a single village, would illustrate, to one who can look below the surface, the same truth. Under the professed uniformity of beliefs, even here in England, what discrepancies and incongruities are concealed! Every type, every individual almost, is distinguished from every other in precisely this point of the judgments he makes about Good. What does the soldier and adventurer think of the life of a studious recluse? or the city man of that of the artist? and vice versa? Behind the mask of good manners we all of us go about judging and condemning one another root and branch. We are in no real agreement as to the worth either of men or things. It is an illusion of the 'canting moralist' (to use Stevenson's phrase) that there is any fixed and final standard of Good. Good is just what any one thinks it to be; and one man has as much right to his opinion as another."

"But," I objected, "it surely does not follow that because there are different opinions about Good, they are all equally valuable."

"No. I should infer rather that they are all equally worthless."

"That does not seem to me legitimate either; and I venture to doubt whether you really believe it yourself."

"Well, at any rate I am inclined to think I do."

"In a sense perhaps you do; but not in the sense which seems to me most important. I mean that when it comes to the point, you act, and are practically bound to act, upon your opinion about what is good, as though you did believe it to be true."

"How do you mean 'practically bound'?"

"I mean that it is only by so acting that you are able to introduce any order or system into your life, or in fact to give it to yourself any meaning at all. Without the belief that what you hold to be good really somehow is so, your life, I think, would resolve itself into mere chaos."

"I don't see that."

"Well, I may be wrong, but my notion is that what systematizes a life is choice; and choice, I believe, means choice of what we hold to be good."

"Surely not! Surely we may choose what we hold to be bad."

"I doubt it."

"But how then do you account for what you call bad men?"

"I should say they are men who choose what I think bad but they think good."

"But are there not men who deliberately choose what they think bad, like Milton's Satan—'Evil be thou my Good'?"

"Yes, but by the very terms of the expression he was choosing what he thought good; only he thought that evil was good."

"But that is a contradiction."

"Yes, it is the contradiction in which he was involved, and in which I believe everyone is involved who chooses, as you say, the Bad. To them it is not only bad, it is somehow also good."

"Does that apply to Nero, for example?"

"Yes, I think it very well might; the things which he chose, power and wealth and the pleasures of the senses, he chose because he thought them good; if his choice also involved what he thought bad, such as murder and rapine and the like (if he did think these bad, which I doubt), then there was a contradiction not so much in his choice as in its consequences. But even if I were to admit that he and others have chosen and do choose what they believe to be bad, it would not affect the point I want to make. For to choose Bad must be, in your view, as absurd as to choose Good ; since, I suppose, you do not believe, that our opinions about the one have any more validity than our opinions about the other. So that if we are to abandon Good as a principle of choice, it is idle to say we may fall back upon Bad."

"No, I don't say that we may ; nor do I see that we must. We do not need either the one or the other. You must have noticed—I am sure I have—that men do not in practice choose with any direct reference to Good or Bad ; they choose what they think will bring them pleasure, or fame, or power, or, it may be, barely a livelihood."

"But believing, surely, that these things are good?"

"Not necessarily ; not thinking at all about it, perhaps."

"Perhaps not thinking about it as we are now ; but still, so far believing that what they have chosen is good, that if you were to go to them and suggest that, after all, it is bad they would be seriously angry and distressed."

"But, probably," interposed Audubon, "like me, they could not help themselves. We are none of us free, in the way you seem to imagine. We have to choose the best we can, and often it is bad enough."

"No doubt," I replied, "but still, as you say yourself, what we choose is the best we can, that is, the most good we can. The criterion is Good, only it is very little of it that we are able to realize."

"No," objected Ellis, "I am not prepared to admit that the criterion is Good. You will find that men will frankly confess that other pursuits or occupations are, in their opinion, better than those they have chosen, and that these better things were and are open to themselves, and yet they continue to devote themselves to the worse, knowing it all the time to be the worse."

"But in most cases," I replied, "these better things, surely, are not really 'open' to them, except so far as external circumstances are concerned. They are hampered in their choice by passions and desires, by that part of them which does not choose, but is passively carried away by alien attractions; and the course they actually adopt is the best they can choose, though they see a better which they would choose if they could. The choice is always of Good, but it may be diverted by passion to less Good."

"I don't know," he said, "that that is a fair account of the matter."

"Nor do I. It is so hard to analyse what goes on in one's own consciousness, much more what goes on in other people's. Still, that is the kind of way I should describe my own experience, and I should expect that most people who reflect would agree with me. They would say, I think, that they always choose the best they can, though regretting that they cannot choose better than they do; and it would seem to them, I think, absurd to suggest that they choose Bad, or choose without any reference either to Good or Bad."

"Well," he said, "granting, for the moment, that you are right—what follows?"

"Why, then," I said, "it follows that we are, as I said, 'practically bound' to accept as valid, for the moment at least, our opinions about what is good; for otherwise we should have no principle to choose by, if it be true that the principle of choice is Good."

"Very well," he said, "then we should have to do without choosing!"

"But could we?"

"I don't see why not; many people do."

"But what sort of people? I mean what sort of life would it be?"

Ellis was preparing to answer when we were interrupted by a voice from behind. The place in which we were sitting opened at the back into one of those large lofty barns which commonly form part of a Swiss house; and as the floor of this room was covered with straw, it was possible to approach that way without making much noise. For this reason, two others of our party had been able to join us without our observing it. Their names were Parry and Leslie; the former a man of thirty, just getting into practice at the Bar, the latter still almost a boy in years, though a very precocious one, whom I had brought with me, ostensibly as a pupil, but really as a companion. He was an eager student of philosophy, and had something of that contempt of youth for any one older than twenty-five, which I can never find it in my heart to resent, though I have long passed the age which qualifies me to become the object of it. He it was who was speaking, in a passionate way he had, when anything like a philosophic discussion was proceeding.

"Why," he was saying, in answer to my last remark, "without choice one would be a mere slave of passion, a creature of every random mood and impulse, a beast, a thing, not a man at all!"

Ellis looked round rather amused.

"Well," he said, "you fire-eater, and why not? I don't know that impulse is such a bad thing. A good impulse is better than a bad calculation any day!"

"Yes, but you deny the validity of the distinction between Good and Bad, so it's absurd for you to talk about a good impulse."

"What *is* your position, Ellis?" asked Parry. "I've been trying in vain to make head or tail of it."

"Why should I take a position at all?" rejoined Ellis. "I protest against this bullying."

"But you *must* take a position," cried Leslie, "if we are to discuss."

"I don't see why; you might take one instead."

"Yes, but you began."

"Well," he conceded, "anything to oblige you. My position, then, to go back again to the beginning, is this. Seeing that there are so many different opinions about what things are good, and that no criterion has been discovered for testing these opinions——"

"My dear Ellis," interrupted Parry, "I protest

against all that from the very beginning. For all practical purposes there is a substantial agreement about what is good."

"My dear Parry," retorted Ellis, "if I am to state a position, let me state it without interruption. Considering, as I was saying, that there are so many different opinions about what things are good, and that no criterion has been discovered for testing them, I hold that we have no reason to attach any validity to these opinions, or to suppose that it is possible to have any true opinions on the subject at all."

"And what do you say to that?" asked Parry, turning to me.

"I said, or rather I suggested, for the whole matter is very difficult to me, that in spite of the divergency of opinions on the point, and the difficulty of bringing them into harmony, we are nevertheless practically bound, whether we can justify it to our reason or not, to believe that our own opinions about what is good have somehow some validity."

"But how 'practically bound'?" asked Leslie.

"Why, as I was trying to get Ellis to admit when you interrupted—and your interruption really completed my argument—I imagine it to be impossible for us not to make choices; and in making choices, as I think, we use our ideas about Good as a principle of choice."

"But you must remember," said Ellis, "that I have never admitted the truth of that last statement."

"But," I said, "if you do not admit it generally—and generally, I confess, I do not see how it could be proved or disproved, except by an appeal to every individual's experience—do you not admit it in your own case? Do you not find that, in choosing, you follow your idea of what is good, so far as you can under the limitations of your own passions and of external circumstances?"

"Well," he replied, "I wish to be candid, and I am ready to admit that I do."

"And that you cannot conceive yourself as choosing otherwise? I mean that if you had to abandon as a principle of choice your opinion about Good, you would have nothing else to fall back upon?"

"No; I think in that case I should simply cease to choose."

"And can you conceive yourself doing that? Can you conceive yourself living, as perhaps many men do, at random and haphazard, from moment to moment, following blindly any impulse that may happen to turn up, without any principle by which you might subordinate one to the other?"

"No," he said, "I don't think I can."

"That, then," I said, "is what I meant, when I suggested that you, at any rate, and I, and other people like us, are practically bound to believe that our opinions about what is good have some validity, even though we cannot say what or how much."

"You say, then, that we have to accept in practice what we deny in theory?"

"Yes, if you like. I say, at least, that the consequence of the attempt to bring our theoretical denial to bear upon our practice would be to reduce our life to a moral chaos, by denying the only principle of choice which we find ourselves actually able to accept. In your case and mine, as it seems, it is our opinion about Good that engenders order among our passions and desires ; and without it we should sink back to be mere creatures of blind impulse, such as perhaps in fact, many men really are."

"What!" cried Audubon, interrupting in a tone of half indignant protest, "do you mean to say that it is some idea about Good that brings order into a man's life? All I can say is that, for my part, I never once think, from one year's end to another, of anything so abstract and remote I simply go on, day after day, plodding the appointed round, without reflexion, without reason, simply because I have to. There's order in my life, heaven knows! but it has nothing to do with ideas about Good. And altogether," he ejaculated, in a kind of passion, "it's a preposterous thing to tell me that I believe in Good, merely because I lead a life like a mill-horse! That would be an admirable reason for believing in Bad—but Good!"

He lapsed again into silence; and I was half unwilling to press him further, knowing that he felt our dialectics to be a kind of insult to his concrete woes. However, it seemed to be necessary for the sake of the argument to give some answer, so I began :—

"But if you don't like the life of a mill-horse, why do you lead it?"

"Why? because I have to!' he replied; "you don't suppose I would do it if I could help it?"

"No," I said, "but why can't you help it?"

"Because," he said, "I have to earn my living."

"Then is it a good thing to earn your living?"

"No, but it's a necessary thing."

"Necessary, why?"

"Because one must live."

"Then it is a good thing to live?"

"No, it's a very bad one."

"Why do you live, then?"

"Because I can't help it."

"But it is always possible to stop living."

"No, it isn't."

"But why not?"

"Because there are other people dependent on me, and I don't choose to be such a mean skunk as to run away myself and leave other people here to suffer. Besides, it's a sort of point of honour. As I'm here, I'm going to play the game. All I say is that the game is not worth the playing; and you will never persuade me into the belief that it is."

"But, my dear Philip," I said, "there is no need for me to persuade you, for it is clear that you are persuaded already. You believe, as you have really admitted in principle, that it is good to live rather than to die; and to live, moreover, a monotonous, laborious life, which you say you detest. Take away that belief, and your whole being is transformed. Either you change your manner of life, abandon the routine which you hate, break up the order imposed (as I said at first) by your idea about Good, and give yourself up to the chaos of chance desires; or you depart from life altogether, on the hypothesis that that is the good thing to do. But in any case the truth appears to remain that somehow or other you do believe in Good; and that it is this belief which determines the whole course of your life."

"Well," he said, "it's no use arguing the point, but I am unconvinced." And he sank back to his customary silence. I thought it useless to pursue the subject with him; but Ellis took up the argument.

"I agree with Audubon," he said. "For even if I admitted your general contention, I should still maintain that it is not by virtue of any conscious idea of Good that we introduce order into our lives. We simply find ourselves, as a matter of fact, by nature and character, preferring one object to another, suppressing or developing this or that tendency. Our choices are not determined by our abstract notion of Good; on the contrary, our notion of Good is deduced from our choices."

"You mean, I suppose, that we collect from our particular choices our general idea of the kind of things which we consider good. That may be. But the point I insist upon is that we do attach validity to these choices; they are, to us, our choices of our Good, those that we approve as distinguished from those that we do not. And my contention is that, in spite of all diversity of opinions as to what really are the good things to choose, we are bound to attach, each of us, some validity to our own, under penalty of reducing our life to a moral chaos."

"But what do you mean by 'validity'?" asked Leslie. "Do you mean that we must believe that our opinions are right?"

"Yes," I said, "or, at least, if not that they are right, that they are the rightest we can attain to for the time being, and until we see something righter. But above all, that opinions on this subject really are either right or wrong, or more right and less right; and that of this rightness or wrongness we really have some kind of perception, however difficult it may be to give an account of it, and that in accordance with such perception we may come to change our opinions or those of other people, by the methods of discussion and persuasion and the like. And all this, as I understand, is what Ellis was denying."

"Certainly," said Ellis, "I was; and I still do not see that you have proved it."

"No," I said, "I have not even tried to. I have only tried to show that in spite of your denial you really do believe it, because a belief in it is implied in all your practical activity. And that, I thought, you did admit yourself."

"But even so," he replied, "it remains to be considered whether my theory is not more reasonable than my practice."

"Perhaps," I replied; "but that, I admit, is not the question that really interests me. What I want to get at is the belief which underlies the whole life of people like ourselves, and of which, it seems, we cannot practically divest ourselves. And such a belief, I think, is this which we have been discussing as to the validity of our opinions about Good."

"I see," he said; "in fact you are concerning yourself not with philosophy but with psychology."

"If you like; it matters little what you call it. Only, whatever it be, you will do me a service if for the moment you will place yourself at my standpoint, and see with me how things look from there."

"Very well," he said, "I have no objection, and so far, on the whole, I do agree with you; though I am bound to point out that you might easily find an opponent less complaisant. Your argument is very much one *ad hominem*."

"It is," I said, "and that, I confess, is the only kind of argument in which I much believe in these matters. I am content, for the present, if you and the others here go along with me."

"I do," said Parry, "but you seem to me to be only stating, in an unnecessarily elaborate way, what after all is a mere matter of common sense."

"Perhaps it is," I replied, "though I have always thought myself rather deficient in that kind of sense. But what does Leslie say?"

"Oh," he said, "I can't think how you can be content with anything so lame and impotent! Some method there must be, absolute and *à priori*, by which we may prove for certain that Good is, and discover, as well, what things are good."

"Well," I said, "if there be such a method, you, if anyone, should find it; and I wish you from my heart good luck in the quest. It is only in default of anything better that I fall back on this—I dare not call it method; this appeal to opinion and belief."

"And even so," said Ellis, "it is little enough that you have shown, or rather, that I have chosen to admit. For even if it were granted that individuals, in order to choose, must believe in Good, it doesn't follow that they believe in anything except each a

Good for himself. So that, even on your own hypothesis, all we could say would be that there are a number of different and perhaps incompatible Goods, each good for some particular individual, but none necessarily good for all. I, at least, admit no more than that."

"How do you mean?" I asked, "for I am getting lost again."

"I mean," he replied, "something that I should have thought was familiar enough. Granted that there really is a Good which each individual ought to choose, and does choose, if you like, as far as he can see it; or granted, at least, that he is bound to believe this, under penalty of reducing his life to moral chaos; still, I see no reason to suppose that the thing which one individual ought to choose is identical, or even compatible, with that which another ought to choose. There may be a whole series of distinct and mutually exclusive moral worlds. In other words, even though I may admit a Good for each, I am not prepared to admit a Good for all."

"But then," I objected, "each of these Goods will also be a not-Good; and that seems to be a contradiction."

"Not at all," he replied, "for each of them only professes to be Good for me, and that is quite compatible with being Bad for another."

"But," cried Leslie, trembling with excitement, "your whole conception is absurd. Good is simply Good; it is not Good for anybody or anything; it is Good in its own nature, one, simple, immutable eternal."

"It may be," replied Ellis, "but I hope you will not actually tear me to pieces if I humbly confess that I cannot see it. I see no reason to admit any such Good; it even has no meaning to me."

"Well, anyhow, nothing else can have any meaning!"

"But, to me, something else has a meaning."

"Well, what?"

"Why, what I have been trying, apparently without success, to explain."

"But don't you see that each of those things you call Goods, oughtn't to be called Good at all, but each of them by some other particular name of its own?"

"Oh, I don't want to quarrel about names; but I call each of them Good because from one point of view—that of some particular individual—each of them is something that ought to be. I, at any rate, admit no more than that. For each individual there is something that ought to be; but this, which ought to be for him, is very likely something that ought not to be for somebody else."

On this Leslie threw himself back with a gesture of digust and despair; and I took the opportunity of intervening.

"Let us have some concrete instances," I said, "of these incompatible Goods."

"By all means," he replied, "nothing can be simpler. It is good, say, for Nero, to preserve supreme power; but it is bad for the people who come in his way. It is good for an American millionaire to make and increase his fortune; but it is bad for the people he ruins in the process. And so on, *ad infinitum;* one has only to look at the world to see that the Goods of individuals are not only diverse but incompatible one with another."

"Of course," I said, "it is true that people do hold things to be good which are in this way mutually incompatible. But does not the fact of this incompatibility make one suspect that perhaps the things in question are not really good?"

"It may, in some cases, but I see no ground for the suspicion. It may very well be that what is good for me is in the nature of things incompatible with what is good for you."

"I don't say it may not be so; but does one believe it to be so? Doesn't one believe that what is really good for one must somehow be compatible with what is really good for others?"

"Some people may believe it, but many don't; and it can never be proved."

"No; and so I am driven back upon my argument *ad hominem*. Do not you, as a matter of fact, believe it?"

"No, I don't know that I do."

"Do you believe then that there is nothing which is good for people in general?"

"I don't see what is to prevent my believing it."

"But, at any rate you do not act as if you believed it."

"In what way do I not?"

"Why, for instance, you said last night that you intended to enter Parliament."

"Well?"

"And in a few weeks you will be making speeches all over the country in favour of—well, I don't quite know what—shall we say in favour of the war?"

"Say so, by all means, if you like."

"And this war, I presume, you believe to be a good thing?"

"Well?"

"Good, that is, not merely for yourself but for the world at large? or at least for the English or the Boers, or one or other of them? Do you admit that?"

"Oh," he said, "I am nothing if not frank! At present, we will admit, I think the war a good thing (whatever that may mean); but what of that? Very probably I am wrong."

"Very probably you are; but that is not the point. The main thing is, that you admit that it is possible to be wrong or right at all; that there is something to be wrong or right about."

"But I don't know that I do admit it, or, at any rate, that I shall always admit it. Probably, after changing my opinions again and again, I shall come to the conclusion that none of them are worth anything at all; that, in fact, there's nothing to have an opinion about; and then I shall retire from politics altogether; and then—then how will you get hold of me?"

"Oh," I replied, "easily enough! For you will still continue, I suppose, to do some kind of work, and work which will necessarily affect innumerable people besides yourself; and you will believe, I presume, that somehow or other the work you do is contributing to some general Good?"

"'You presume'! you do indeed presume! Suppose I believe nothing of the kind? Suppose I deny altogether a general Good?"

"We will suppose it, if you like," I said. "And now let us go on to examine the consequences of the supposition."

"By all means!" he said, "proceed!"

"Well," I began, "since you are still living in society, (for that, I suppose, you allow me to assume,) you are, by the nature of the case, interchanging with others innumerable offices. At the same time, on the supposition we are adopting, that you deny a general Good, your only object in this interchange will be your own Good, (in which you admit that you do believe.) If, for example, you are a doctor, your aim, at the highest, is to develop yourself, to increase your knowledge, your skill, your self-control; at the lowest, it is to accumulate a fortune; but in neither case can your purpose be to alleviate or cure disease, nor to contribute to the advance of science; for that would be to suppose that these ends, although they purport to be general, nevertheless are somehow good, which is the hypothesis we were excluding. Similarly, if you are a lawyer, you will not set your heart on doing justice, or perfecting the law; such ends as these for you are mere illusions; for even if justice exist at all, it certainly is not a Good, for if it were, it would be a Good for all, and, as we agree, there is no such thing. Men like Bentham, therefore, to you will be mere visionaries, and the legal system as a whole will have no sense or purport, except so far as it contributes to sharpen your wits and fill your pocket. And so, in general, with all professions and occupations; whichever you may adopt, you will treat it merely as a means to your own Good; and since you have no Good which is also common to other men, you will use these others without scruple to further what you conceive to be your own advantage, without necessarily paying any regard to what they may conceive to be theirs."

"Well," he said, "and why not?"

"I don't ask 'why not'?" I replied, "I ask merely whether it would be so? whether you do, as a matter of fact, conceive it possible that you should ever adopt such an attitude?"

"Well, no," he admitted, "I don't think it is; but that is an idiosyncrasy of mine; and I have no doubt there are plenty of other men who are precisely in the position you describe. Take, for example, a man like the late Jay Gould. Do you suppose that he, in his business operations, ever had any regard for anything except his own personal advantage? Do you suppose he cared how many people he ruined? Do you suppose he cared even whether he ruined his country, except so far as such ruin might interfere with his own profit? Or look again at the famous Mr. Leiter of Chicago! What do you suppose it mattered to him that he might be starving half the world, and imperilling the governments of Europe? It was enough for him that he should realize a fortune; of all the rest, I suppose, he washed his hands. He and men like him adopt, I have no doubt, precisely the position which you are trying to show is impossible."

"No," I said, "I am not trying to show that it is impossible in general; I am only trying to show that it is impossible for you. And my object is to suggest that if a man does deny a general Good, he denies it, as I say, at his peril. If his denial is genuine, and not merely verbal, it will lead him to conduct of the kind I have described."

"But surely," interrupted Leslie, "you have no right to assume that a disbelief in a general Good, however genuine, necessarily involves a sheer egoism in conduct? For a man might find that his own Good consisted in furthering the Good of other people; and in that case of course he will try to further it."

"But," I replied, "on our hypothesis there is no Good of other people. Each individual, we agreed, has his Good, but there is no Good common to all. And thus we could have no guarantee that in furthering the Good of one we are also furthering that of others. So that even supposing a man to believe that his own Good consists in furthering the Good of others, yet he will not be able to put his belief into practice, but at most will be able to help some one man, with the likelihood that in so doing he is thwarting and injuring many others. Though, therefore, he may not wish to be an egoist, yet he cannot work for a common Good; and that simply because there is no common Good to work for."

At this point Parry, who had been sitting silent during the discussion, probably because of its somewhat abstract character, suddenly broke in upon it as follows. He had a great fund of optimism and what is sometimes called common sense, which to me was rather pleasant and refreshing, though some of the others, and especially Leslie and Ellis, were apt, I think, to find it irritating. His present speech was characteristic of his manner.

"Ah!" he began, "there you touch upon the point which has vitiated your argument throughout. You seem to assume that because every man has his own Good, and there is no Good we can affirm to be common to all, therefore these individual Goods are incompatible one with another, so that a man who is intent on his own Good is necessarily hindering, or, at least, not helping, other people who are intent on theirs. But I believe, and my view is borne out by all experience, that exactly the opposite is the case. Every man, in pursuing his own advantage, is also enabling the rest to pursue theirs. The world, if you like to put it so, is a world of egoists; but a world constructed with such exquisite art, that the egoism of one is not only compatible with, but indispensable to that of another. On this principle all society rests. The producer, seeking his own profit, is bound to satisfy the consumer; the capitalist cannot exist without supporting the labourer; the borrower and lender are knit by the closest ties of mutual advantage; and so with all the ranks and divisions of mankind, social, political, economic, or what you will. Balanced, one against the other, in delicate counterpoise, in subtlest interaction of part with part, they sweep on in one majestic system, an equilibrium for ever disturbed, yet ever recovering itself anew, created, it is true, and maintained by countless individual impulses, yet summing up and reflecting all of these in a single, perfect, all-harmonious whole. And when we consider——"

But here he was interrupted by a kind of groan from Audubon; and Ellis, seeing his opportunity, broke in ironically, as follows:

"The theme, my dear Parry, is indeed a vast one, and suggests countless developments. When, for example, we consider (to borrow your own phrase) the reciprocal relations of the householder and the thief, of the murderer and his victim, of the investor and the fraudulent company-promoter; when, turning from these private examples, we cast our eyes on international relations, when we observe the perfect accord of interest between all the great powers in the far East; when we note the smooth harmonious working of that flawless political machine so aptly named the European Concert, each member pursuing its own advantage, yet co-operating without friction to a common end; or when, reverting to the economic sphere, we contemplate the exquisite adjustment that prevails between the mutual interest of labour and capital—an adjustment broken only now and again by an occasional disturbance, just to show that the centre of gravity is changing; when we observe the World Trust quietly, without a creak or a groan, annihilating the individual producer; or when, to take the sublime example which has already been quoted, we perceive a single individual, in the pursuit of his own Good, positively co-operating with revolutionists on the other side of the globe, and contributing, by the process of starvation, to the deliverance of a great and oppressed people—if indeed, in such a world as ours, anyone can be said to be oppressed—when, my dear Parry, we contemplate these things, then—then—words fail me! Finish the sentence as you only can!"

"Oh," said Parry, good-naturedly enough, "of course I know very well you can make anything ridiculous if you like. But I still maintain that we must take broad views of these matters, and that the position adopted is substantially correct, if you take long enough periods of time. Every man in the long run by pursuing his own Good does contribute also to the Good of others."

"Well," I said, anxious to keep the argument to the main point, "let us admit for the moment that it is so. You assert, then, that everyone's Good is distinct from everyone else's, and that there is no common Good; but that each one's pursuit of his own Good is essential to the realization of the Good of all the rest."

"Yes," he said; "roughly, that is the kind of thing I believe."

"Well, but," I continued, "on that system there is at least one thing which we shall have to call a common Good."

"And what is that?"

"Society itself! For society is the condition indispensable to all alike for the realization of any individual Good; and a common condition of Good is, I suppose, in a sense, a common Good."

"Yes," he replied, "I suppose, in a sense, it is."

"Well," I said, "I want no larger admission. For under 'society' what is not included! Sanction society, and you sanction, or at least you admit the possibility of a sanction for every kind of common activity and end; and the motives of men in undertaking these common activities become a matter of comparative indifference. Whatever they are consciously aiming at, whether it be their own Good, or the Good of all, or, as is more probable, a varying mixture of both, the fact remains that they do, and we do, admit a common Good, the maintenance and development of society itself. And that is all I was concerned to get you to agree to."

"But," said Leslie, "do you really think that there is no common Good except this, which you yourself admit to be rather a condition of Good than Good itself?"

"No," I replied, "that is not my view. I do not, myself, regard society as nothing but a condition of the realization of independent, individual Goods. On the contrary, I think that the Good of each individual consists in his relations with other individuals. But this I do not know that I am in a position to establish. Meantime, however, we can, I think, maintain, that few candid men, understanding the issue, will really deny altogether a common Good; for they will have to admit that in society we have at the very least a common condition of Good."

"But still," objected Leslie, "even so we have no proof that there is a common Good, but only that most civilized men, if pressed, would probably admit one."

"Certainly," I replied, "and I pretend nothing more. I have not attempted to prove that there is a common Good, nor even that it is impossible not to believe in one. I merely wished to show, as before, that if a man disbelieves, he disbelieves, so to speak, at his own peril. And to sum up the argument, what I think we have shown is, that to deny a common Good is, in the first place, to deny to one's life and action all worth except what is bound up with one's own Good, to the complete exclusion of any Good of all. In the second place, it is to deny all worth to every public and social institution—to religion, law, government, the family, all activities, in a word, which contribute to and make up what we call society. Further, it is to empty history, which is the record of society, of its main interest and significance, and in particular to eliminate the idea of progress ; for progress, of course, implies a common Good towards which progress is directed. In brief, it is to strip a man of his whole social self, and reveal him a poor, naked, shivering Ego, implicated in relations from which he may derive what advantage he can for himself, but which, apart from that advantage, have no point or purport or aim ; it is to make him an Egoist even against his will ; leaving him for his solitary ideal a cult of self-development, deprived of its main attraction by its dissociation from the development of others. Now, if any man, having a full sense of what is implied in his words (a sense, not merely conceived by the intellect, but felt, as it were, in every nerve and tissue) will seriously and deliberately deny that he believes in a common Good ; if he will not merely make the denial with his lips, but actually carry it out in his daily life, adjusting to his verbal proposition his habitual actions, feelings, and thoughts; if he will and can really and genuinely do this, then I, for my part, am willing to admit that I cannot prove him to be wrong. All I can do is to set my experience against his, and to appeal to the experience of others; and we must wait till further experience on either side leads (if it ever is to lead) to an agreement. But, on the other hand, if a man merely makes the denial with his lips, because, perhaps, he conceives it impossible to prove the opposite, or because he sees that what is good cannot be defined beyond dispute, or whatever other plausible reason he may have ; and if, while he persists in his denial, he continues to act as if the contrary were true, taking part with zest and enthusiasm in the common business of life, pushing causes, supporting institutions, subscribing to societies, and the like, and that without any pretence that in so doing he is seeking merely his own Good—in that case I shall take leave to think that he does not really believe what he says (though no doubt he may genuinely think he does), and I shall take his life and his habits, the whole tissue of his instincts and desires, as a truer index to his real opinion than the propositions he enunciates with his lips."

"But," cried Leslie, "that is a mere appeal to prejudice! Of course we all want to believe that there is a common Good; the question is, whether we have a right to."

"Perhaps," I replied, "but the question I wished to raise was the more modest one, whether we can help it? Whether we have a right or no is another matter, more difficult and more profound than I care to approach at present. If, indeed, it could be proved beyond dispute to the reason, either that certain things are good or that they are not, there would be no place for such discussions as this. But, it appears, such proof has not yet been given,—or do you think it has?"

"No!" he said, "but I think it might be and must be!"

"Possibly," I said, "but meantime, perhaps, it is wiser to fall back on this kind of reasoning which you call an appeal to prejudice,—and so no doubt in a sense it is; for it is an appeal to the passion men have to find worth in their lives, and their refusal to accept any view by which such worth is denied. To anyone who refuses to accept any judgment about what is good, I prove, or endeavour to prove, that such refusal cuts away the whole basis of his life; and I ask him if he is prepared to accept that consequence. If he affirms that he is, and affirms it not only with his lips but in his action, then I have no more to say; but if he cannot accept the consequences, then, I suppose, he will reconsider the premisses, and admit that he does really believe that judgments about what is good may be true, and, provisionally, that his own are true, or at least as true as he can make them, and that he does in fact accept and act upon them as true, and intends to do so until he is convinced that they are false. And this attitude of his feelings, you may call, if you like, an attitude of faith; it is, I think, the attitude most men would adopt if they were pressed home upon the subject; and to my mind it is reasonable enough, and rather to be praised than to be condemned."

"I don't think so at all," cried Leslie, "I consider it very unsatisfactory."

"So do I," said Parry, "and for my part, I can't see what you're all driving at. You seem to be making a great fuss about nothing."

"Oh no!" retorted Ellis, "not about nothing! about a really delightful paradox! We have arrived at the conclusion that we are bound to believe in Good, but that we haven't the least notion what it is!"

"Exactly!" said Parry, "and that is just what I dispute!"

"What? That we are bound to believe in Good?"

"No! But that we don't know what Good is, or rather, what things are good."

"Oh!" I cried, "do you really think we do know? I wish I could think that! The trouble with me is, that while I seem to see that we are bound to trust our judgments about what is good, yet I cannot see that we know that they are true. Indeed, from their very diversity, it seems as if they could not all be true. My only hope is, that perhaps they do all contain some truth, although they may contain falsehood as well."

"But surely," said Parry, "you exaggerate the difficulty. All the confusion seems to me to arise from the assumption that we can't see what lies under our noses. I don't believe, myself, that there is all this difficulty in discovering Good. Philosophers always assume, as you seem to be doing, that it is all a matter of opinion and reasoning, and that opinions and reasons really determine conduct. Whereas in fact, I believe, conduct is determined, at least in essentials, by something very much more like instinct. And it is to this instinct which, by the nature of the case, is simple and infallible, that we ought to look to tell us what is good, and not to our reason, which, as you admit yourself, can only land us in contradictory judgments. I know, of course, that you have a prejudice against any such view."

"Not at all!" I said, "if only I could understand it. I should be glad of any simple and infallible criterion; only I have never yet been able to find one."

"That, I believe, is because you look for it in the wrong place; or, perhaps, because you look for it instead of simply seeing it. You will never discover what is good by any process of rational inquiry. It's a matter of direct perception, above and beyond all argument."

"Perhaps it is," I said, "but surely not of perception, as you said, simple and infallible?"

"If not that, at least sufficiently clear and distinct for all practical purposes. And to my mind, all discussion about Good is for this reason rather factitious and unreal. I don't mean to say, of course, that it isn't amusing, among ourselves, to pass an hour or two in this kind of talk; but I should think it very unfortunate if the habit of it were to spread among the mass of men. For inquiry does tend in the long run to influence opinion, and generally to influence it in the wrong way; whereas, if people simply go on following their instinct, they are much more likely to do what is right, than if they try to act on so-called rational grounds."

"But," cried Leslie, who during this speech had found obvious difficulty in containing himself, "what is this instinct which you bid us follow? What authority has it? What validity? What is its content? What *is* it, anyhow, that it should be set up in this way above reason?"

"As to authority," replied Parry, "the point about an instinct is, that its authority is unimpeachable. It commands and we obey; there's no question about it."

"But there *is* question about the content of Good."

"I should rather say that we make question. But, after all, how small a part of our life is affected by our theories! As a rule, we act simply and without reflection; and such action is the safest and most prosperous."

"The safest and most prosperous! But how do you know that? What standard are you applying? Where do you get it from?"

"From common sense."

"And what is common sense?"

"Oh, a kind of instinct too!"

"A kind of instinct? How many are there then? And does every instinct require another to justify it, and so *ad infinitum*?"

"Logomachy, my dear Leslie!" cried Parry, with imperturbable good-humour. He had a habit of treating Leslie as if he were a clever child.

"But really, Parry," I interposed, "this is the critical point. Is it your view that an instinct is its own sufficient justification, or does it require justification by something else?"

"No," he said, "it justifies itself. Take, for example, a strong instinct, like that of self-preservation. How completely it stands above all criticism! Not that it cannot be criticised in a kind of dilettante, abstract way; but in the moment of action the criticism simply disappears in face of the overwhelming fact it challenges."

"Do you mean to say, then," said Leslie, "that because this instinct is so strong therefore it is always good to follow it?"

"I should say so, generally speaking."

"How is it, then, that you consider it disgraceful that a man should run away in battle?"

"Ah!" replied Parry, "that is a very interesting point! There you get a superposition of the social upon the merely individual instinct."

"And how does that come about?"

"That may be a matter of some dispute; but it has been ingeniously explained as follows. We start with the primary instinct of self-preservation. This means, at first, that each individual strives to preserve himself. But as time goes on individuals discover that they can only preserve themselves by associating with others, and that they must defend society if they want to defend themselves. They thus form a habit of defending society; and this habit becomes in time a second instinct, and an instinct so strong that it even overrides the primary one from which it was derived; till at last you get individuals sacrificing in defence of the community those very lives which they originally entered the community to preserve."

"What a charming paradox!" cried Ellis. "And so it is really true that every soldier who dies on the field of battle does so only by virtue of a miscalculation? And if he could but pull himself up and remember that, after all, the preservation of his life was the only motive that induced him to endanger it, he would run away like a sensible man, and try some other device to achieve his end, the device of society having evidently broken down, so far as he is concerned."

"There you are again," said Parry, "with your crude rationalism! The point is that the social habit has now become an instinct, and has therefore, as I say, imperative authority! No operations of the reason touch it in the least."

"Well," rejoined Ellis, "I must say that it seems to me very hard that a man can't rectify such an important error. The imposition is simply monstrous! Here are a number of fellows shut up in society on the distinct understanding, to begin with, that society was to help them to preserve their lives; instead of which, it starves them and hangs them and sends them to be shot in battle, and they aren't allowed to raise a word of protest or even to perceive what a fraud is being perpetrated upon them!"

"I don't see that it's hard at all," replied Parry; "it seems to me a beautiful device of nature to ensure the predominance of the better instincts."

"The better instincts!" I cried, "but there is the point! These instincts of yours, it seems, conflict; in battle, for example, the instinct to run away conflicts with the instinct to stay and fight?"

"No doubt," he admitted.

"And sometimes one prevails and sometimes the other?"

"Yes."

"And in the one case we say that the man does right, when he stays and fights; and in the other that he does wrong, when he runs away?"

"I suppose so."

"Well, then, how does your theory of instincts help us to know what is Good? For it seems that after all we have to choose between instincts, to approve one and condemn another. And our problem still remains, how can we do this? how can we get any certainty of standard?"

"Perhaps the faculty that judges is itself an instinct?"

"Perhaps it is," I replied, "I don't really know what an instinct is. My quarrel is not with the word instinct, but with what seemed to be your assumption that whatever it is in us that judges about Good judges in a single, uniform, infallible way. Whereas, in fact, as you had to admit, sometimes at the same moment it pronounces judgments not only diverse but contradictory."

"But," he replied, "those seem to me to be exceptional cases. As a rule the difficulty doesn't occur. When it does, I admit that we require a criterion. But I should expect to find it in science rather than in philosophy."

"In science!" exclaimed Leslie. "What has science to do with it?"

"What has *not* science to do with?" said a new voice from behind. It was Wilson who, in his turn, had joined us from the breakfast room (he always breakfasted late), and had overheard the last remark. He was a lecturer in Biology at Cambridge, rather distinguished in that field, and an enthusiastic believer in the capacity of the scientific method to solve all problems.

"I was saying," Leslie repeated in answer to his question, "that science has nothing to do with the Good."

"So much the worse for the Good," rejoined Wilson, "if indeed that be true."

"But you, I suppose, would never admit that it is," I interposed. I was anxious to hear what he had to say, though at the same time I was desirous to avoid a discussion between him and Leslie, for their types of mind and habits of thought were so radically opposed that it was as idle for them to engage in debate as for two bishops of opposite colour to attempt to capture one another upon a chessboard. He answered readily enough to my challenge.

"I think," he said, "that there is only one method of knowledge, and that is the method we call scientific."

"But do you think there is any knowledge of Good at all, even by that method? or that there is nothing but erroneous opinions?"

"I think," he replied, "that there is a possibility of knowledge, but only if we abjure dialectics. Here, as everywhere, the only safe guide is the actual concrete operation of Nature."

"How do you mean?" asked Leslie, his voice vibrating with latent hostility.

"I mean that the real significance of what we call Good is only to be ascertained by observing the course of Nature; Good being in fact identical with the condition towards which she tends, and morality the means to attaining it."

"But——" Leslie was beginning, when Parry cut him short.

"Wait a moment!" he said. "Let Wilson have a fair hearing!"

"This end and this means," continued Wilson, "we can only ascertain by a study of the facts of animal and human evolution. Biology and Sociology, throwing light back and forward upon one another, are rapidly superseding the pseudo-science of Ethics."

"Oh dear!" cried Ellis, *sotto-voce*, "here comes the social organism! I knew it would be upon us sooner or later."

"And though at present, I admit," proceeded Wilson, not hearing, or ignoring, this interruption, "we are hardly in a position to draw any certain conclusions, yet to me, at least, it seems pretty clear what kind of results we shall arrive at."

"Yes!" cried Parry, eagerly, "and what are they?"

"Well," replied Wilson, "I will indicate, if you like, the position I am inclined to take up, though of course it must be regarded as provisional."

"Of course! Pray go on!"

"Well," he proceeded, "biology, as you know, starts with the single cell——"

"How do you spell it?" said Ellis, with shameless frivolity, "with a C or with an S?"

"Of these cells," continued Wilson, imperturbably, "every animal body is a compound or aggregation; the aggregation involving a progressive modification in the structure of each cell, the differentiation of groups of cells to perform special functions,—digestive, respiratory, and the rest,—and the subordination of each cell or group of cells to the whole. Similarly, in sociology——"

"Dear Wilson," cried Ellis, unable any longer to

contain himself, "mightn't we take all this for granted?"

"Wait a minute," I said, "let him finish his analogy."

"That's just it!" cried Leslie, "it's nothing but an analogy. And I don't see how——"

"Hush, hush!" said Parry. "Do let him speak!"

"I was about to say," continued Wilson, "when I was interrupted, that in the social organism——"

"Ah!" interjected Ellis, "here it is!"

"In the social organism, the individual corresponds to the cell, the various trades and professions to the organs. Society has thus its alimentary system, in the apparatus of production and exchange; its circulatory system, in the network of communications; its nervous system, in the government machinery; its——"

"By the bye," interrupted Ellis, "could you tell me, for I never could find it in Herbert Spencer, what exactly in society corresponds to the spleen?"

"Or the liver?" added Leslie.

"Or the vermiform appendix?" Ellis pursued.

"Oh, well," said Wilson, a little huffed at last, "if you are tired of being serious it's no use for me to continue."

"I'm sorry, Wilson!" said Ellis. "I won't do it again; but one does get a little tired of the social organism."

"More people talk about it," answered Wilson, "than really understand it."

"Very true," retorted Ellis, "especially among biologists."

At this point I began to fear we should lose our subject in polemics; so I ventured to recall Wilson to the real issue.

"Supposing," I said, "that we grant the whole of your position, how does it help us to judge what is good?"

"Why," he said, "in this way. What we learn from biology is, that it is the constant effort of nature to combine cells into individuals and individuals into societies—the protozoon, in other words, evolves into the animal, the animal into what some have called the 'hyper-zoon,' or super-organism. Well, now, to this physical evolution corresponds a psychical one. What kind of consciousness an animal may have, we can indeed only conjecture; and we cannot even go so far as conjecture in the case of the cell; but we may reasonably assume that important psychical changes of the original elements are accompaniments and conditions of their aggregation into larger entities; and the morality (if you will permit the word) of the cell that is incorporated in an animal body will consist in adapting itself as perfectly as may be to the new conditions, in subordinating its consciousness to that of the Whole—briefly, in acquiring a social instead of an individual self. And now, to follow the clue thus obtained into the higher manifestations of life. As the cell is to the animal, so is the individual to society, and that on the psychical as well as on the physical side. Nature has perfected the animal; she is perfecting society; that is the end and goal of all her striving. When, therefore, you raise the question, what is Good, biology has this simple answer to give you: Good is the perfect social soul in the perfect social body."

As he concluded, Ellis exclaimed softly, "'*Parturiunt montes*,'" and Leslie took it up with: "And not even a mouse!"

"Whether it is a mouse or no," I said, "it would be hard to say, until we had examined it more closely. At present it seems to me more like a cloud, which may or may not conceal the goddess Truth. But the question I really want to ask is, What particular advantage Wilson gets from the biological method? For the conclusion itself, I suppose, might have been reached, and commonly is, without any recourse to the aid of natural science."

"No doubt," he said, "but my contention is, that it is only by the scientific method that you get proof. You, for example, may assert that you believe the social virtues ought to prevail over individual passions; but if your position were challenged, I don't see how you would defend it. Whereas I can simply point to the whole evolution of Nature as tending towards the Good I advocate; and can say:—if you resist that tendency you are resisting Nature herself!"

"But isn't it rather odd," said Ellis, "that we should be able to resist Nature?"

"Not at all," he replied, "for our very resistance is part of the plan; it's the lower stage persisting into the higher, but destined sooner or later to be absorbed."

"I see," I said, "and the keynote of your position is, as you said at the beginning, that Good is simply what Nature wants. So that, instead of looking within to find our criterion, we ought really to look without, to discover, if we can, the tendency of Nature and to acquiesce in that as the goal of our aspiration."

"Precisely," he replied, "that is the position."

"Well," I said, "it is plausible enough; but the plausibility, I am inclined to think, comes from the fact that you have been able to make out, more or less, that the tendency of Nature is in the direction which, on the whole, we prefer."

"How do you mean?"

"Well," I said, "supposing your biological researches had led you to just the opposite conclusion, that the tendency of Nature was not from the cell to the animal, and from the individual to society, but in precisely the reverse direction, so that the end of all things was a resolution into the primitive elements—do you think you would have been as ready to assert that it is the goal of Nature that must determine our ideal of Good?"

"But why consider such a hypothetical case?"

"I am not so sure," I replied, "that it is more hypothetical than the other. At any rate it is a hypothesis adopted by one of your authorities. Mr. Herbert Spencer, you will remember, conceives the process of Nature to be one, not, as you appear to think, of continuous progress, but rather of a circular movement, from the utmost simplicity to the utmost complexity of Being, and back again to the original condition. What you were describing is the movement which we call upward, and which we can readily enough believe to be good, at any rate upon a superficial view of it. But now, suppose us to have reached the point at which the opposite movement begins; suppose what we had to look forward to and to describe as the course of Nature were a process, not from simple to complex, from homogeneous to heterogeneous, or whatever the formula may be, but one in exactly the contrary direction, a dissolution of society into its individuals, of animals into the cells of which they are composed, of life into chemistry, of chemistry into mechanism, and so on through the scale of Being, reversing the whole course of evolution—should we, in such a case, still have to say that the process of Nature was right, and that she is to give the law to our judgment about Good?"

"Yes," he replied, "I think we should; and for this reason. Only those who do on the whole approve the course of Nature have the qualities enabling them to survive; the others will, in the long run, be eliminated. There is thus a constant tendency to harmonize opinions with the actual process of the world; and that, no doubt, is why we approve what you call the upward movement, which is the one in which Nature is at present engaged. But, for the same reason, if, or when, a movement in the opposite direction should set in, people holding opinions like ours will tend to be eliminated, while those will tend to survive more and more who approve the current of evolution then prevailing."

"And in this way," said Ellis, "an exquisite unanimity will be at last attained, by the simple process of eliminating the dissentients!"

"Precisely!"

"Well," cried Leslie, "no doubt that will be very satisfactory for the people who survive; but it does not help us much. What we want to know is, what *we* are to judge to be Good, not what somebody else will be made to judge, centuries hence."

"And for my part," said Ellis, "I'm not much impressed by the argument you attribute to Nature, that if we don't agree with her we shall be knocked on the head. I, for instance, happen to object strongly to her whole procedure: I don't much believe in the harmony of the final consummation—even if it were to be final, and not merely the turn of the tide; and I am sensibly aware of the horrible discomfort of the intermediate stages, the pushing, kicking, trampling of the host, and the wounded and dead left behind on the march. Of all this I venture to disapprove; then comes Nature and says, 'but you ought to approve!' I ask why, and she says, 'Because the procedure is mine.' I still demur, and she comes down on me with a threat—'Very good, approve or no, as you like; but if you don't approve you will be eliminated!' 'By all means,' I say, and cling to my old opinion with the more affection that I feel myself invested with something of the glory of a martyr. Nature, it seems, is waiting for me round the corner because I venture to stick to my principles. 'Ruat cælum!' I cry; and in my humble opinion it's Nature, not I, that cuts a poor figure!"

"My dear Ellis," protested Wilson, "what's the use of talking like that? It's not really sublime, it's only ridiculous!"

"Certainly!" retorted Ellis; "it's you who are sublime. I prefer the ridiculous."

"So," I said, "does Wilson, if one may judge by appearances. For I cannot help thinking he is really laughing at us."

"Not at all," he replied, "I am perfectly serious."

"But surely," I said, "you must see that any discussion about Good must turn somehow upon our perception of it? The course of Nature may, as you say, be good; but Nature cannot be the measure of Good; the measure can only be Good itself; and the most that the study of Nature could do would be to illuminate our perception by giving it new material for judgment. Judge we must, in the last resort; and the judgment can never be a mere statement as to the course which Nature is pursuing."

"Well," said Wilson, "but you will admit at least the paramount importance of the study of Nature, if we are ever to form a right judgment?"

"I feel much more strongly," I replied, "the importance of the study of Man; however, we need not at present discuss that. All that I wanted to insist upon was, that the contention which you have been trying to sustain, that it is possible, somehow or other, to get rid of the subjectivity of our judgments about Good by substituting for them a statement about the tendencies of Nature—that this contention cannot be upheld."

"If that be so," he said, "I don't see how you are ever to get a scientific basis for your judgment."

"I don't know," I replied, "that we can. It depends upon what you include under science."

"Oh," he said, "by science I mean the resumption in brief formulæ of the sequence of phenomena; or, more briefly, a description of what happens."

"If that be so," I replied, "the method of judging about Good can certainly not be scientific; for judgments about Good are judgments of what ought to be, not of what is."

"But then," objected Wilson, "what method is left you? You have nothing to fall back upon but a chaos of opinions."

"But might there not be some way of judging between opinions?"

"How should there be, in the absence of any external objective test?"

"What do you mean by that?"

"Why," he replied, "the kind of test which you have in the case of the sciences. They depend, in the last resort, not on ideas of ours, but on the routine of common sense-perception; a routine which is independent of our choice or will, but is forced upon us from without with an absolute authority such as no imaginings of our own can impugn. Thus we get a certainty upon which, by the power of inference, whose mechanism we need not now discuss, we are able to build up a knowledge of what is. But when, on the other hand, we turn to such of our ideas as deal with the Good, the Beautiful, and the like—here we have no test external to ourselves, no authority superior and independent. Invite a group of men to witness a scientific experiment, and none of them will be able to deny either the sequence of the phenomena produced, or the chain of reasoning (supposing it to be sound) which leads to the conclusion based upon them. Invite the same men to judge of a picture, or consult them on a question of moral casuistry, and they will propound the most opposite opinions; nor will there be any objective test by which you can affirm that one opinion is more correct than another. The deliverances of the external sense are, or at least can be made, by correction of the personal equation, infallible and the same for all; those of the internal sense are different not only in different persons, but in the same person at different times."

"Yes," said Leslie, impatiently, "we have all admitted that! The question is whether——"

"Excuse me," Wilson interposed, "I haven't yet come to my main point. I was going to say that not merely are there these differences of opinion, but even if there were not, even if the opinions were uniform, they would still, as opinions, be subjective and devoid of scientific validity. It is the external reference that gives its certainty to science; and such a reference is impossible in the case of judgments about the Beautiful and the Good. Such judgments are merely records of what we think or feel. These ideas of ours may or may not happen to be consistent one with another; but whether they are so or not, they are merely our ideas, and have nothing to do with the essential nature of reality."

"I am not sure," I replied, "that the distinction really holds in the way in which you put it. Let us take for a moment the point of view of God—only for the sake of argument," I added, seeing him about to protest. "God, we will suppose, knows all Being through and through as it really is; and along with this knowledge of reality he has a conviction that reality is good. Now, with this conviction of his none other, *ex hypothesi*, can compete; for he being God, we must at any rate admit that if anybody can be right, it must be he. No one then can dispute or shake his opinion; and since he is eternal he will not change it of himself. Is there then, under the circumstances, any distinction of validity between his judgment that what is, is, and his judgment that what is, is good?"

"I don't see the use," he replied, "of considering such an imaginary case. But if you press me I can only say that I still adhere to my view that any judgment about Good, whether made by God or anybody else, can be no more than a subjective expression of opinion."

"But," I rejoined, "in a sense, all certainty is subjective, in so far as the certainty has to be perceived. It is impossible to eliminate the Subject. In the case, for example, upon which you dwelt, of the impressions of external sense, the certainty of the impressions is your and my certainty that we have them; and so in the case of a cogent argument; for any given person the test of the cogency is his perception that the cogency is there. And it is the same with the Beautiful and the Good; there is no conceivable test except perception. Our difficulty here is simply that perceptions conflict; not that we have no independent test. But if, as in the case I imagined, the perception of Good was harmonious with itself, then the certainty on that point would be as final and complete as the certainty in the proof of a proposition of Euclid."

"I am afraid," said Wilson, "I don't follow you. You're beginning to talk metaphysics."

"Call it what you will," I replied, "so long only as it is sense."

"No doubt," he said, "but I don't feel sure that it is."

"In that case you can show me where I am wrong."

"No," he replied, "for, as I said, I can't follow you."

"He means he won't," said Ellis, breaking in with his usual air of an unprejudiced outsider, "But after all, what does it really matter? Whatever the reason may be for our uncertainty as to Good, the fact remains that we are uncertain. There's my Good, thy Good, his Good, our Good, your Good, their Good; and all these Goods in process of flux, according to the time of day, the time of life, and the state of the liver. That being so, what is the use of discussing Good in itself? And why be so disturbed about it? There's Leslie, for instance, looking as if the bottom were knocked out of the universe because he can't discover his objective standard! My dear boy, life goes on just the same, my life, his life, your life, all the lives. Why not make an end of the worry at once by admitting frankly that Good is a chimæra, and that we get on very well without it?"

"But I don't get on well without it!" Leslie protested.

"No," I said, "and I hoped that by this time we were agreed that none of us could. But Ellis is incorrigible."

"You don't suppose," he replied, "that I am going to agree with you merely because you override me in argument—even if you did, which you don't."

"But at least," cried Leslie, "you needn't tell us so often that you disagree."

"Very well," he said, "I am dumb." And for a moment there was silence, till I began to fear that our argument would collapse; when, to my relief, Parry returned to the charge.

"You will think me," he began, "as obstinate as Ellis; but I can't help coming back to my old point of view. Somehow or other, I feel sure you are making a difficulty which the practical man does not really feel. You object to my saying that he knows what is good by instinct; but somehow or other I am sure that he does know it. And what I suggest now is, that he finds it written in experience."

"In whose experience?" Leslie asked defiantly.

"In that of the race, or, at least, in that of his own age and country. Now, do be patient a moment, and let me explain! What I want to suggest is, that every civilization worth the name possesses, in its laws and institutions, in the customs it blindly follows, the moral code it instinctively obeys, an actual objective standard, worked out in minute detail, of what, in every department of life, really is good. To this standard every plain man, without reasoning, and even without reflexion, does in fact simply and naturally conform; so do all of us who are discussing here, in all the common affairs of our daily life. We know, if I may say so, better than we know; and the difficulties into which we are driven, in speculations such as that upon which we are engaged, arise, to my mind, from a false and unnecessary abstraction—from putting aside all the rich content of actual life, and calling into the wilderness for the answer to a question which solves itself in the street and the market-place."

"Well," I said, "for my own part, I am a good deal in sympathy with what you say. At the same time there is a difficulty."

"A difficulty!" cried Leslie, "there are hundreds and thousands!"

"Perhaps," I replied, "but the particular one to which I was referring is this. Every civilization, no doubt, has its own standard of Good; but these standards are different and even opposite; so that it would seem we require some criterion by which to compare and judge them."

"No," cried Parry, "that is just what I protest against. We are not concerned with other ideals than our own. Every great civilization believes in itself. Take, for instance, the ancient Greeks, of whom you are so fond of talking. In my opinion they are absurdly over-estimated; but they had at least that good quality—they believed in themselves. To them the whole non-Greek world was barbarian; the standard of Good was frankly their own standard; and it was a standard knowable and known, however wide might be the deviations from it in practice. We find accordingly that for them the ideal was rooted in the real. Plato, even, in constructing his imaginary republic, does not build in the void, evoking from his own consciousness a Cloud-Cuckoo-city for the Birds; on the contrary, he bases his structure upon the actual, following the general plan of the institutions of Sparta and Crete; and neither to him nor to Aristotle does it ever occur that there is, or could be, any form of state worth considering, except the city-state with which they were familiar. It is the same with their treatment of ethics; their ideal is that of the Greeks, not of Man in general, and stands in close relation to the facts of contemporary life. So, too, with their art; it is not, like that of our modern romanticists, an impotent yearning for vaguely-imagined millenniums. On the contrary, it is an ideal interpretation of their own activity, a mirror focussing into feature and form the very same fact which they saw distorted and blurred in the troubled stream of time. The Good, in the Greek world, was simply the essence and soul of the Real; and the Socrates of Xenophon who frankly identified justice with the laws, was only expressing, and hardly with exaggeration, the current convictions of his countrymen. That, to my mind, is the attitude of health; and it is the one natural to the plain man in every well-organized society. Good is best known when it is not investigated; and people like ourselves would do no useful service if we were to induce in others the habit of discussion which education has made a second nature to ourselves."

"My dear Parry!" cried Ellis, "you alarm me! Is it possible that we are all anarchists in disguise?"

"Parry," I observed, "seems to agree with the view attributed by Browning to Paracelsus, that thought is disease, and natural health is ignorance."

"Well," rejoined Ellis, "there is a good deal to be said for that."

"There's a good deal to be said for everything," I rejoined. "But if thought indeed be disease, we must recognise the fact that we are suffering from it; and so, I fear, is the whole modern world. It was easy for the Greeks to be 'healthy'; practically they had no past. But for us the past overweights the present; we cannot, if we would, get rid of the burden of it. All that was once absolute has become relative, including our own conceptions and ideals; and as we look back down the ages and see civilization after civilization come into being, flourish and decay, it is impossible for us to believe that the society in which we happen to be born is more ultimate than any of these, or that its ideal, as reflected in its institutions, has any more claim than theirs to be regarded as a final and absolute expression of Good."

"Well," said Parry, "let us admit, if you like, that ideals evolve, but, in any case, the ideal of our own time has more validity for us than any other. As to those of the past, they were, no doubt, important in their day, but they have no importance for the modern world. The very fact that they are past is proof that they are also superseded."

"What!" cried Leslie, indignantly, "do you mean to say that everything that is later in time is also better? That we are better artists than the Greeks? better citizens than the Romans? more spiritual than the men of the Middle Ages? more vigorous than those of the Renaissance?"

"I don't know," replied Parry, "that I am bound to maintain all that. I only say that on the whole I believe that ideals progress; and that therefore it is the ideals of our own time, and that alone, which we ought practically to consider."

"The ideal of our own time?" I said, "but which of them? there are so many."

"No, there is really only one, as I said before; the one that is embodied in current laws and customs."

"But these are always themselves in process of change."

"Yes, gradual change."

"Not necessarily gradual; and even if it were, still change. And to sanction a change, however slight, may always mean, in the end, the sanctioning of a whole revolution."

"Besides," cried Leslie, "even if there were anything finally established, what right have we to judge that the established is the Good?"

"I don't know that we have any right; but I am sure it is what we do."

"Perhaps we do, many of us," I said, "but always, so far as we reflect, with a lurking sense that we may be all wrong. Or how else do you account for the curious, almost physical, sinking and disquiet we are apt to experience in the presence of a bold denier?"

"I don't know that I do experience it."

"Do you not? I do so often; and only yesterday I had a specially vivid experience of the kind."

"What was that?"

"Well, I was reading Nietzsche."

"Who is he?"

"A German writer. It does not much matter, but I had him in my mind when I was speaking."

"Well, but what does he say?"

"It's not so much what he says, as what he denies."

"What does he deny, then?

"Everything that you, I suppose, would assert. I should conjecture, at least, that you believe in progress, democracy, and all the rest of it."

"Well?"

"Well, he repudiates all that. Everything that you would reckon as progress, he reckons as decadence. Democracy he regards, with all that it involves, as a revolt of the weak against the strong, of the bad against the good, of the herd against the master. Every great society, in his view, is aristocratic, and aristocratic in the sense that the many are deliberately and consciously sacrificed to the few; and that, not as a painful necessity, but with a good conscience, in free obedience to the universal law of the world. 'Be strong, be hard' are his ultimate ethical principles. The modern virtues, or what we affect to consider such, sympathy, pity, justice, thrift, unselfishness and the like, are merely symptoms of moral degeneration. The true and great and noble man is above all things selfish; and the highest type of humanity is to be sought in Napoleon or Cæsar Borgia."

"But that's mere raving!"

"So you are pleased to say; and so, indeed, it really may be. But not simply because it contradicts those current notions which we are embodying, as fast as we can, in our institutions. It is precisely those notions that it challenges; and it is idle to meet it with a bare denial."

"I can conceive no better way of meeting it!"

"Perhaps, for purposes of battle. Yet, even so, you would surely be stronger if you had reason for your faith."

"But I think my reason sufficient—those are not the ideas of the age."

"But for all you know they may be those of the next."

"Well, that will be its concern."

"But surely, on your own theory, it must also be yours; for you said that the later was also the better. And the better, I suppose, is what you want to attain."

"Well!"

"Well then, in supporting the ideas and institutions generally current, you may be hindering instead of helping the realization of the Good you want to achieve."

"But I don't believe Nietzsche's ideas ever could represent the Good!"

"Why not?"

"Because I don't."

"But, at any rate, do you abandon the position that we can take the ideas of our time as a final criterion?"

"I suppose so—I don't know—I'm sure there's something in it! Do you believe yourself that they have no import for us?"

"I didn't say that; but I think we have to find what the import is. We cannot substitute for our own judgment the mere fact of a current convention, any more than we can substitute the mere fact of the tendency of Nature. For, after all, it is the part of a moral reformer to modify the convention. Or do you not think so?"

"Perhaps," he admitted, "it may be!"

"Perhaps it may be!" cried Leslie, "but palpably

it is! Is there any institution or law or opinion you could name which is not open to obvious criticism? Take what you will—parliamentary government, the family, the law of real property—is there one of them that could be adequately and successfully defended?"

"Certainly!" began Parry, with some indignation. "The family——"

"Oh," I interrupted, "we are not yet in a position to discuss that! But upon one thing we seem to be agreed—that whatever may be the value of current standards of Good in assisting our judgment, we cannot permit them simply to supersede it by an act of authority. And so once more we are thrown back each upon his own opinions."

"To which, according to you," interposed Parry, "we are bound to attach some validity."

"And yet which we are aware," added Ellis, "cannot possibly have any."

I was about to protest against this remark when I saw, coming round from the garden, Bartlett and Dennis, the two remaining members of our party. They had just returned from a mountaineering expedition; and now, having had their bath, had come out to join us in our usual place of assembly. Bartlett had in his hand the *Times* and the *Daily Chronicle*. He was a keen business man, and a Radical politician of some note; and though not naturally inclined to speculative thought, would sometimes take part in our discussions if ever they seemed to touch on any practical issue. On these occasions his remarks were often very much to the point; but his manner being somewhat aggressive and polemic, his interposition did not always tend to make smooth the course of debate. It was therefore with mingled feelings of satisfaction and anxiety that I greeted his return. After some talk about their expedition, he turned to me and said, "We ought to apologise, I suppose, for interrupting a discussion?"

"Not at all!" I replied; "but, as you are here, perhaps you will be willing to help us?"

"Oh," he said, "I leave that to Dennis. This kind of thing isn't much in my line."

"What kind of thing?" Leslie interjected. "I don't believe you even know what we're talking about!"

"Talking about. Why, philosophy, of course! What else should it be when you get together?"

"This time," I said, "it's not exactly philosophy, but something more like ethics."

"What is the question?" asked Dennis.

Dennis was always ready for a discussion, and the more abstract the theme, the better he was pleased. He had been trained for the profession of medicine, but coming into possession of a fortune, had not found it necessary to practise, and had been devoting his time for some years past to Art and Metaphysics. I always enjoyed talking to him, though the position he had come to hold was one which I found it very difficult to understand, and I am not sure that I have been able to represent it fairly.

"We have been discussing," I said, in answer to his question, "our judgments about what is good, and trying without much success to get over the difficulty, that whereas, on the one hand, we seem to be practically obliged to trust these judgments, on the other we find it hard to say which of them, if any, are true, and how far and in what sense."

"Oh," he replied, "then Bartlett ought really to be able to help you. At any rate he's very positive himself about what's good and what's bad. Curiously enough, he and I have been touching upon the same point as you, and I find, among other things, that he is a convinced Utilitarian."

"I never said so," said Bartlett, "but I have no objection to the word. It savours of healthy homes and pure beer!"

"And is that your idea of Good?" asked Leslie, irritated, as I could see, by this obtrusion of the concrete.

"Yes," he replied, "why not? It's as good an idea as most."

"I suppose," I said, "all of us here should agree that the things you speak of are good. But somebody might very well deny it."

"Of course somebody can deny anything, if only for the sake of argument."

"You mean that no one could be serious in such a denial?"

"I mean that everybody really knows perfectly well what is good and what is bad; the difficulty is, not to know it, but to do it!"

"But surely you will admit that opinions do differ?"

"They don't differ nearly so much as people pretend, on important points; or, if they do, the difference is not about what ought to be done, but about how to do it."

"What ought to be done, then?" asked Leslie defiantly.

"Well, for example we ought to make our cities decent and healthy."

"Why?"

"Because we ought; or, if you like, because it will make people happy."

"But I don't like at all! I don't see that it's necessarily good to make people happy."

"Oh well, if you deny that——"

"Well, if I deny that?"

"I don't believe you to be serious, that's all. Good simply means, what makes people happy; and you must know that as well as I do."

"You see!" interposed Dennis; "I told you he was a Utilitarian."

"I daresay I am; at any rate, that's what I think; and so, I believe, does everybody else."

"'The Universe,'" murmured Ellis, "'so far as sane conjecture can go, is an immeasurable swine's trough, consisting of solid and liquid, and of other contrasts and kinds; especially consisting of attainable and unattainable, the latter in immensely greater quantities for most pigs.'"

"That's very unfair," Parry protested, "as an account of Hedonism."

"I don't see that it is at all," cried Leslie.

"I think," I said, "that it represents Bentham's position well enough, though probably not Bartlett's."

"Oh well," said Parry, "Bentham was only an egoistic Hedonist."

"A what?" said Bartlett.

"An egoistic Hedonist."

"And what may that be?"

"An egoistic Hedonist," Parry was beginning, but Ellis cut him short. "It's best explained," he said, "by an example. Here, for example, is Bentham's definition of the pleasures of friendship; they are, he says, 'those which accompany the persuasion of possessing the goodwill of such and such individuals, and the right of expecting from them, in consequence, spontaneous and gratuitous services.'"

We all laughed, though Parry, who loved fair play, could not help protesting. "You really can't judge," he said, "by a single example."

"Can't you?" cried Ellis; "well then, here's another. 'The pleasures of piety' are 'those which accompany the persuasion of acquiring or possessing the favour of God; and the power, in consequence, of expecting particular favours from him, either in this life or in another.'"

We laughed again; and Parry said, "Well, I resign myself to your levity. And after all, it doesn't much matter, for no one now is an egoistic Hedonist."

"What are we then," asked Bartlett, "you and I?"

"Why, of course, altruistic Hedonists," said Parry.

"And what's the difference?"

"The difference is," Parry began to explain, but Ellis interrupted him again.

"The difference is," he cried, "that one is a brute and the other a prig."

"Really, Ellis," Parry began in a tone of remonstrance.

"But, Parry," I interposed, "are you a Utilitarian?"

"Not precisely," he replied; "but my conclusions are much the same as theirs. And of all the *à priori* systems I prefer Utilitarianism, because it is at least clear, simple, and precise."

"That is what I can never see that it is."

"Why, what is your difficulty?"

"In the first place," I said, "the system appears to rest upon a dogma."

"True," he said, "but that particular dogma—the greatest happiness of the greatest number—is one which commends itself to everyone's consciousness."

"I don't believe it!" said Ellis. "Let us take an example. A crossing-sweeper, we will suppose, is suffering from a certain disease about which the doctors know nothing. Their only chance of discovering how to cure it is to vivisect the patient; and it is found, by the hedonistic calculus, that if they do so, a general preponderance of pleasure over pain will result. Accordingly, they go to the crossing-sweeper and say, 'O crossing-sweeper! In the name of the utilitarian philosophy we call upon you to submit to vivisection. The tortures you will have to endure, it is true, will be inconceivable: but think of the result! A general preponderance in the community at large of pleasure over pain! For every atom of pain inflicted on you, an atom of pleasure will accrue to somebody else. Upon you, it is true, will fall the whole of the pain; whereas the pleasure will be so minutely distributed among innumerable individuals that the increment in each case will be almost imperceptible. No matter, it will be there! and our arithmetic assures us that the total gain in pleasure will exceed the total loss in pain. It will also be distributed among a greater number of individuals. Thus all the requirements of the hedonistic calculus are satisfied! Your duty lies plain before you! Rise to the height of your destiny, and follow us to the dissecting room!' What do you think the crossing-sweeper would say? I leave it to Bartlett to express his sentiments!"

"My dear Ellis," said Parry, "your example is absurd. The case, to begin with, is one that could not possibly occur. And even if it did, one could not expect the man who was actually to suffer, to take an impartial view of the situation."

"But," I said, "putting the sufferer out of the question, what would really be the opinion of the people for whom he was to suffer? Do you think they would believe they ought to accept the sacrifice? Every man, I think, would repudiate it with horror for himself; and what right has he to accept it for other people?"

"On the utilitarian hypothesis," said Parry, "he certainly ought to."

"No doubt; but would he? Utilitarianism claims to rest upon common sense, but, in the case adduced, I venture to think common sense would repudiate it."

"Perhaps," he said, "but the example is misleading. It is a case, as I said, that could not occur—a mere marginal case."

"Still," I said, "a marginal case may suggest a fundamental fallacy. Anyhow, I cannot see myself that the judgment that the greatest happiness of the greatest number is good has a more obvious and indisputable validity than any other judgments of worth. It seems to me to be just one judgment among others; and, like the others, it may be true or false. However, I will not press that point. But what I should like to insist upon is, that the doctrine which Bartlett seemed to hold——"

"I hold no doctrine," interrupted Bartlett; "I merely expressed an opinion, which I am not likely to change for all the philosophy in the world." And with that he opened the *Chronicle*, and presently becoming absorbed, paid for some time no further attention to the course of our debate.

"Well," I continued, "the doctrine, whether Bartlett holds it or no, that the ultimately good thing is the greatest happiness of the greatest number, cannot be insisted upon as one which appeals at once to everyone's consciousness as true, so that, in fact, since its enunciation, the controversy about Good may be regarded as closed. It will hardly be maintained, I imagine, even by Parry, that the truth of the doctrine is a direct and simple intuition, so that it has only to be stated to be accepted?"

"Certainly not," Parry replied, "the contention of the Utilitarians is that everyone who has the capacity and will take the trouble to reflect will, in fact, arrive at their conclusions."

"The conclusions being like other conclusions about what is good, the result of a difficult process of analysis, in which there are many possibilities of error, and no more self-evident and simple than any other judgment of the kind?"

He agreed.

"And further, the general principle, tentative and uncertain as it is, requiring itself to be perpetually interpreted anew for every fresh case that turns up."

"How do you mean?"

"Why," I said, "even if we grant that the end of action is the greatest happiness of the greatest number, yet we have still to discover wherein that happiness consists."

"But," he said, "happiness we define quite simply as pleasure."

"Yes; but how do we define pleasure?"

"We don't need to define it. Pleasure and pain are simply sensations. If I cut my finger, I feel pain; if I drink when I am thirsty, I feel pleasure. There can be no mistake about these feelings; they are simple and radical."

"Undoubtedly. But if you limit pleasure and pain to such simple cases as these, you will never get out of them a system of Ethics. And, on the other hand, if you extend the terms indefinitely, they lose at once all their boasted precision, and become as difficult to interpret as Good and Evil."

"How do you mean?"

"Why," I said, "if all conduct turned on such simple choices as that between thick soup and clear, then perhaps its rules might be fairly summed up in the utilitarian formula. But in fact, as everyone knows, the choices are far more difficult; they are between, let us say, a bottle of port and a Beethoven symphony; leisure and liberty now, or £1000 a-year twenty years hence; art and fame at the cost of health, or sound nerves and obscurity; and so on, and so on through all the possible cases, infinitely more complex in reality than I could attempt to indicate here, all of which, no doubt, could be brought under your formula, but none of which the formula would help to solve."

"Of course," said Parry, "the hedonistic calculus is difficult to apply. No one, that I know of, denies that."

"No one could very well deny it," I replied. "But now, see what follows. Granting, for the moment, for the sake of argument, that in making these difficult choices we really do apply what you call the hedonistic calculus——"

"Which I, for my part, altogether deny!" cried Leslie.

"Well,' I resumed, "but granting it for the moment, yet the important point is not the criterion, but the result. It is a small thing to know in general terms (supposing even it were true that we do know it) that what we ought to seek is a preponderance of pleasure over pain; the whole problem is to discover, in innumerable detailed cases, wherein precisely the preponderance consists. But this can only be learnt, if at all, by long and difficult, and, it may be, painful experience. We do not really know, *à priori*, what things are pleasurable, in the extended sense which we must give to the word if the doctrine is to be at all plausible, any more definitely than we know what things are good. And the Utilitarians by substituting the word Pleasure for the word Good, even if the substitution were legitimate, have not really done much to help us in our choice."

"But," he objected, "we do at least know what Pleasure is, even if we do not know what things are pleasurable."

"And so I might say we do know what Good is, even if we do not know what things are good."

"But we know Pleasure by direct sensation."

"And so I might say we know Good by direct perception."

"But you cannot define Good."

"Neither can you define Pleasure. Both must be recognised by direct experience."

"But, at any rate," he said, "there is this distinction, that in the case of Pleasure everyone *does* recognise it when it occurs; whereas there is no such general recognition of Good."

"That," I admitted, "may, perhaps, be true; I am not sure."

"But," broke in Leslie, "what does it matter whether it be true or no? What has all this to do with the question? It's immaterial whether Pleasure or Good is the more easily and generally recognisable. The point is that they are radically different things."

"No," objected Parry, "*our* point is that they are the same thing."

"But I don't believe you really think so, or that anyone can."

"And *I* don't believe that anyone can*not*!"

"Do you mean to say that you really agree with Bentham that, quantity of pleasure being equal, pushpin is as good as poetry?"

"Yes; at least I agree with what he means, though the particular example doesn't appeal to me, for I hardly know what either pushpin or poetry is."

"Well then, let us take Plato's example. Do you think that, quantity of pleasure being equal, scratching oneself when one itches is as good as, say, pursuing scientific research."

"Yes. But of course the point is that quantity of pleasure is not equal."

"You mean," interposed Ellis, "that there is more pleasure in scratching?"

"No, of course not."

"But at least you will admit that there is more pleasure in some physical experiences? Plato, for example, takes the case of a catamite."

"I admit nothing of the kind. In the first place, these gross physical pleasures do not last."

"But suppose they did? Imagine an eternal, never-changing bliss of scratching, or of——"

"I don't see the use of discussing the matter in this kind of way. It seems to me to deserve serious treatment."

"But I am perfectly serious. I do genuinely believe that a heaven of scratching, or at any rate of some analogous but intenser experience, would involve an indefinitely greater sum of pleasure than a heaven of scientific research."

"Well, all I can say is, I don't agree with you."

"But why not?" cried Leslie. "If you were candid I believe you would. The fact is that you have predetermined that scientific research is a better thing than such physical pleasure, and then you bring out your calculation of pleasure so as to agree with that foregone conclusion. And that is what the Utilitarians always do. Being ordinary decent people they accept the same values as the rest of the world, and on the same grounds as the rest of the world. And then they pretend, and no doubt believe themselves, that they have been led to their conclusions by the hedonistic calculus. But really, if they made an impartial attempt to apply the calculus fairly, they would arrive at quite different results, results which would surprise and shock themselves, and destroy the whole plausibility of their theory."

"That is your view of the matter."

"But isn't it yours?"

"No, certainly not."

"At any rate," I interposed, "it seems to be clear that this utilitarian doctrine has nothing absolute or final or self-evident about it. All we can say is that among the many opinions about what things are good, there is also this opinion, very widely held, that all pleasurable things are good, and that nothing is good that is not pleasurable. But that, like any other opinion, can be and is disputed. So that we return pretty much to the point we left, that there are a number of conflicting opinions about what things are good, that to these opinions some validity must be attached, but that it is difficult to see how we are to reconcile them or to choose between them. Only, somehow or other, as it seems to me, the truth about Good must be adumbrated in these opinions, and by interrogating the actual experience of men in their judgments about good things, we may perhaps be able to get at least some shadowy notion of the object of our quest."

"And so," said Ellis, getting up and stretching himself, "even by your own confession we end where we began."

"Not quite," I replied. "Besides, have we ended?"

For some minutes it seemed as though we had. The mid-day heat (it was now twelve o'clock) and the silence broken only by the murmur of the fountain (for the mowers opposite had gone home to their dinner) seemed to have induced a general disinclination to the effort of speech or thought. Even Dennis whom I had never known to be tired in body or mind, and who was always debating something—it seemed to matter very little what—even he, I thought at first, was ready to let the discussion drop. But presently it became clear that he was only revolving my last words in his mind, for before long he turned to me and said:

"I don't know what you mean by 'interrogating experience,' or what results you hope to attain by that process." At this Leslie pricked up his ears, and I saw that he at least was as eager as ever to pursue the subject further.

"Why," continued Dennis, "should there not be a method of discovering Good independently of all experience?"

The phrase immediately arrested Wilson's attention.

"'A method independent of experience,'" he cried, "why, what kind of a method would that be?"

"It is not so easy to describe," replied Dennis. "But I was thinking of the kind of method, for example, that is worked out by Hegel in his *Logic*."

"I have never read Hegel," said Wilson. "So that doesn't convey much to my mind."

"Well," said Dennis, "I am afraid I can't summarize him!"

"Can't you?" cried Ellis, "I can! Here he is in a nutshell! Take any statement you like—for example, 'Nothing exists!'—put it into the dialectical machine, turn the handle, and hey presto! out comes the Absolute! The thing's infallible; it does not matter what you put in; you always get out the same identical sausage."

Dennis laughed. "There, Wilson," he said, "I hope you understand now!"

"I can't say I do," replied Wilson, "but I daresay it doesn't much matter."

"Perhaps, then," said Ellis, "you would prefer the Kantian plan."

"What is that?"

"Oh, it's much simpler than the other. You go into your room, lock the door, and close the shutters, excluding all light. Then you proceed to invert the mind, so as to relieve it of all its contents; look steadily into the empty vessel, as if it were a well; and at the bottom you will find Truth in the form of a categorical imperative. Or, if you don't like that, there's the method of Fichte. You take an Ego, by preference yourself; convert it into a proposition; negate it, affirm it, negate it again, and so on *ad infinitum*, until you get out the whole Universe in the likeness of yourself. But that's rather a difficult method; probably you would prefer Spinoza's. You take——"

"No!" cried Dennis, "there I protest! Spinoza is too venerable a name."

"So are they all, all venerable names," said

Ellis. "But the question is, to which of them do you swear allegiance? For they all arrive at totally different results."

"I don't know that I swear allegiance to any of them," he replied. "I merely ventured to suggest that it is only by some such method of pure reason that one can ever hope to discover Good."

"You do not profess then," I said, "to have discovered any such method yourself?"

"No."

"Nor do you feel sure that anyone else has?"

"No."

"You simply lie down and block the road?"

"Yes," he said, "and you may walk over me if you can."

"No," I said, 'it will be simpler, I think, if possible, to walk round you." For by this time an idea had occurred to me.

"Do so," he said, "by all means, if you can."

"Well," I began, "let us suppose for the sake of argument that there really is some such method as you suggest of discovering Good—a purely rational method, independent of all common experience."

"Let us suppose it," he said, "if you are willing."

"Is it your idea then," I continued, "that this Good so discovered, would be out of all relation to what we call goods? Or would it be merely the total reality of which they are imperfect and inadequate expressions?"

"I do not see," he said, "why it should have any relationship to them. All the things we call good may really be bad; or some good and some bad in a quite chaotic fashion. There is no reason to suppose that our ideas about Good have any validity unless it were by an accidental coincidence."

"And further," I said, "though we really do believe there is a Good, and that there is a purely rational and *à priori* method of discovering it, yet we do not profess to have ascertained that method ourselves, nor do we feel sure that it has been ascertained by anyone? In any case, we admit, I suppose, that to the great mass of men, both of our own and all previous ages, such a method has remained unknown and unsuspected?"

He agreed.

"But these men, nevertheless, have been pursuing Goods under the impression that they were really good."

"Yes."

"And in this pursuit they have been expending, great men and small alike, or rather those whom we call great and small, all that store of energy, of passion, and blood and tears which makes up the drama of history?"

"Undoubtedly!"

"But that expenditure, as we now see, was futile and absurd. The purposes to which it was directed were not really good, nor had they any tendency to promote Good, unless it were in some particular case by some fortunate chance. Whatever men have striven to achieve, whether like Christ, to found a religion, or, like Cæsar, to found a polity, whether their quest were virtue or power or truth, or any other of the ends we are accustomed to value and praise, or whether they sought the direct opposites of these, or simply lived from hour to hour following without reflexion the impulse of the moment, in any and every case all alike, great and small, good and bad, leaders and followers, or however else we may class them, were, in fact, equally insignificant and absurd, the idle sport of illusions, one as empty and baseless as another. The history of nations, the lives of individual men, are stripped, in this view, of all interest and meaning; nowhere is there advance or retrogression, nowhere better or worse, nowhere sense or consistency at all. Systems, however imposing, structures, however vast, fly into dust and powder at a touch. The stars fall from the human firmament; the beacon-lights dance like will-o'-the-wisps; the whole universe of history opens, cracks, and dissolves in smoke; and we, from an ever-vanishing shore, gaze with impotent eyes at the last gleam on the wings of the dove of Reason as it dips for ever down to eternal night. Will not that be the only view we can take of the course of human action if we hold that what we believe to be goods have no relation to the true Good?"

"Yes," he admitted, "I suppose it will."

"And if we turn," I continued, "from the past to the present and the future, we find ourselves, I think, in even worse case. For we shall all, those of us who may come to accept the hypothesis you put forward, be deprived of the consolation even of imagining a reason and purpose in our lives. The great men of the past, at any rate, could and did believe that they were helping to realize great Goods; but we, in so far as we are philosphers, shall have to forego even that satisfaction. We shall believe, indeed, that Good exists, and that there is a method of discovering it by pure reason ; but this method, we may safely assume, we shall not most of us have ascertained. Or do you think we shall ? "

" I cannot tell," he said ; " I do not profess to have ascertained it myself."

" And meantime," I said, " you have not even the right to assume that it is a good thing to endeavour to ascertain it. For the pursuit of Truth, it must be admitted, is one of the things which we call good ; and these, we agreed, have not any relation to the true Good. Consider, then, the position of these unfortunate men who have learnt indeed that there is a Good, but who know nothing about it, except that it has nothing to do with what they call good. What kind of life will they live ? Whatever they may put their hand to, they will at once be paralyzed by the thought that it cannot possibly be worth pursuing. Politics, art, pleasure, science—of these and all other ends they know but one thing, that all is vanity. As by the touch of enchantment, their world is turned to dust. Like Tantalus they stretch lips and hands towards a water for ever vanishing, a fruit for ever withdrawn. At war with empty phantoms, they 'strike with their spirit's knife,' as Shelley has it, 'invulnerable nothings.' Dizzy and lost they move about in worlds not only unrealized, but unrealizable, 'children crying in the night, with no language but a cry,' and no father to cry to. And in all this blind confusion the only comfort vouchsafed is that somehow or other they may, they cannot tell how, discover a Good of which the only thing they know is that it has no connection with the Goods they have lost. Is not this a fair account of the condition to which men would be reduced who really did accept and believe your hypothesis?"

"Yes," he said, "perhaps it is, but still I must protest against this appeal to prejudice and passion. Supposing the truth really were as I suggested, we should have to face it, whether or no it seemed to ruin our own life."

"Yes," I agreed, "supposing the truth were so. But, after all, we have no sufficient theoretical reason for believing it to be so, and every kind of practical reason against it. We cannot, it is true, demonstrate—and that was admitted from the first—that any of our judgments about what is good are true; but there is no reason why we should not believe—and I should say we must believe—that somehow or other they do at least have truth in them."

"Well, and if so?"

"If so, we do not depend, as you said we do, or at least we do not believe ourselves to depend, for our knowledge about Good, upon some purely rational process not yet discovered; but those things which we judge to be good really, we think, in some sense or so, and by analyzing and classifying and comparing our experiences of such things we may come to see more clearly what it is in them that we judge to be good; and again by increasing experience we may come to know more Good than we knew; and generally, if we once admit that we have some light, we may hope, by degrees, to get more; and that getting of more light will be the most important business, not only of philosophy, but of life."

"But if we can judge of Good at all, why do we

not judge rightly? If we really have a perception, how is it that it is confused, not clear?"

"I cannot tell how or why; but perhaps it is something of this kind. Our experience, in the first place, is limited, and we cannot know Good except in so far as we experience it—so, at least, I think, though perhaps you may not agree. And if that be so, even if our judgments about Good that we have experienced were clear, our conclusions drawn from them would yet be very imperfect and tentative, because there would be so much Good that we had not experienced. But, in fact, as it seems, our judgments even about what we do experience are confused, because every experience is indefinitely complex, and contains, along with the Good, so much that is indifferent or bad. And to analyze out precisely what it is that we are judging to be good is often a difficult and laborious task, though it is one that should be a main preoccupation with us all."

"You think, then, that there are two reasons for the obscurity and confusion that prevail in our judgments about Good—one, that our experience is limited, the other that it is complex?"

"Yes; and our position in this respect, as it always seems to me, is like that of people who are learning to see, or to develop some other sense. Something they really do perceive, but they find it hard to say what. Their knowledge of the object depends on the state of the organ; and it is only by the progressive perfecting of that, that they can settle their doubts and put an end to their disputes, whether with themselves or with other people."

"How do you mean?"

"Well, if you will allow me to elaborate my metaphor, I conceive that we have a kind of internal sense, like a rudimentary eye, whose nature it is to be sensitive to Good, just as it is the nature of the physical eye to be sensitive to light. But this eye of the soul, being, as I said, rudimentary, does not as yet perceive Good with any clearness or precision, but only in a faint imperfect way, catching now one aspect of it, now another, but never resting content in any of these, being driven on by the impulse to realize itself to ever surer and finer discrimination, with the sense that it is learning its own nature as it learns that of its object, and that it will never be itself a true and perfect organ until it is confronted with the true and perfect Good. And as by the physical eye we learn by degrees to distinguish colours and forms, to separate and combine them, and arrange them in definite groups, and then, going further, after discerning in this way a world of physical things, proceed to fashion for our delight a world of art, in that finer experience becoming aware of our own finer self; so, by this eye of hers, does the soul, by long and tentative effort, learn to distinguish and appraise the Goods which Nature presents to her; and then, still unsatisfied, proceed to shape for herself a new world, as it were, of moral art, fashioning the relations of man to Nature and to his fellow-man under the stress of her need to realize herself, ever creating and ever destroying only to create anew, learning in the process her own nature, yet aware that she has never learnt it, but passing on without rest to that unimagined consummation wherein the impulse that urges her on will be satisfied at last, and she will rest in the perfect enjoyment of that which she knows to be Good, because in it she has found not only her object but herself. Is not this a possible conception?"

"I do not say," he replied, "that it is impossible; but I still feel a difficulty."

"What is it?" I said, "for I am anxious not to shirk anything."

"Well," he said, "you will remember when Parry suggested that the perception of Good might perhaps be an instinct, you objected that instincts conflict one with another, and that we therefore require another faculty to choose between them. Now it seems to me that your own argument is open to the same objection. You postulate some faculty—which perhaps you might as well call an instinct—and this faculty, as I understand you, in the effort to realize itself, proceeds to discriminate various objects as good. But, now, does this same faculty also know that the Goods are good, and which is better than which, and generally in what relations they stand to one another and to the absolutely Good? Or do we not require here, too, another faculty to make these judgments, and must not this faculty, as I said at first, have previously achieved, by some method of its own, a knowledge of Good, in order that it may judge between Goods?"

"No," I said, "in that way you will get, as you hint, nothing but an infinite regress. The perception of Good, whenever it comes, must be, in the last analysis, something direct, immediate, and self-evident; and so far I am in agreement with Parry. My only quarrel with him was in regard to his assumption that the judgments we make about Good are final and conclusive. The experiences we recognize as good are always, it seems to me, also bad; because we are never able to apprehend or experience what is absolutely Good. Only, as I like to believe—you may say I have no grounds for the belief—we are always progressing towards such a Good; and the more of it we apprehend and experience, the more we are aware of our own well-being; or perhaps I ought to say, of the well-being of that part of us, whatever it may be—I call it the soul—which pursues after Good. For her attitude, perhaps you will agree, towards her object, is not simply one of perception, but one of appetency and enjoyment. Her aim is not merely to know Good, but to experience it; so that along with her apprehension of Good goes her apprehension of her own well-being, dependent upon and varying with her relation to that, her object. Thus she is aware of a tension, as it were, when she cannot expand, of a drooping and inanition when nutriment fails, of a rush of health and vigour as she passes into a new and larger life, as she freely unfolds this or that aspect of her complex being, triumphs at last over an obstacle that has long hemmed and thwarted her course, and rests for a moment in free and joyous consciousness of self, like a stream newly escaped from a rocky gorge, to meander in the sun through a green melodious valley. And this perception she has of her own condition is like our perception of health and disease. We know when we are well, not by any process of ratiocination, by applying from without a standard of health deduced by pure thought, but simply by direct sensation of well-being. So it is with this soul of ours, which is conversant with Good. Her perception of Good is but the other side of her perception of her own well-being, for her well-being consists in her conformity to Good. Thus every phase of her growth (in so far as she grows) is in one sense good, and in another bad; good in so far as it is self-expression, bad in so far as the expression is incomplete. From the limitations of her being she flies, towards its expansion she struggles; and by her perception that every Good she attains is also bad, she is driven on in her quest of that ultimate Good which would be, if she could reach it, at once the complete realization of herself, and her complete conformity to Good."

"But," he objected, "apart from other difficulties, in your method of discovering the Good is there no place for Reason at all?"

"I would not say that," I replied, "though I am bound to confess that I see no place for what you call pure Reason. It is the part of Reason, on my hypothesis, to tabulate and compare results. She does not determine directly what is good, but works, as in all the sciences, upon given data, recording the determinations not (in this case) of the outer but of the inner sense, noticing what kinds of activity satisfy, and to what degree, the expanding nature of this soul that seeks Good, and deducing therefrom, so far as may be, temporary rules of conduct based upon that unique and central experience which is the root and foundation of the whole. Temporary rules, I say, because, by the nature of the case, they can have in them nothing absolute and final, inasmuch as they are mere deductions from a process which is always developing and transforming itself. Systems of morals, maxims of conduct are so many landmarks left to show the route by which the soul is marching; casts, as it were, of her features at various stages of her growth, but never the final record of her perfect countenance. And that is why the current morality, the positive institutions and laws, on which Parry insisted with so much force, both have and have not the value he assigned to them. They are in truth invaluable records of experience, and he is rash who attacks them without understanding; and yet, in a sense, they are only to be understood in order to be superseded, because the experience they resume is not final, but partial and incomplete. Would you agree with that, Parry, or no?"

"I am not sure," he said. "It would be a dangerous doctrine to put in practice."

"Yes," I said, "but I fear that life itself is a dangerous thing, and nothing we can do will make it safe. Our only hope is courage and sanity."

"But," said Dennis, "to return to the other point, on your view is our knowledge of Good altogether subsequent to experience?"

"Yes," I replied, "our knowledge is, if you like; but it is a knowledge of experience in Good. We first recognize Good by what I call direct perception; then we analyze and define what we have recognized; and the results of this process, I suppose, is what we call knowledge, so far as it goes."

"And there can be no knowledge of Good independent of experience?"

"I do not know; perhaps there might be; only I should like to suggest that even if we could arrive at such a knowledge by pure reason, we should have achieved only a definition of Good, not Good itself; for Good, I suppose you will agree, must be a state of experience, not a formula."

"Even if it be so," he said, "it might still be possible to arrive at its formula by pure reason."

"It may be so," I replied, "only I console myself with the thought, that if, as is the case with so many of us, we cannot see our way to any such method, we are not left, on my hypothesis, altogether forlorn. For though we cannot know Good, we can go on realizing Goods, and so making progress towards the ultimate Good, which is the goal not merely of knowledge but of action."

"And how, may I ask," said Wilson, after a pause, "in your conception, is Good related to Happiness?"

"That," I replied, "is one of the points we have to ascertain by experience. For I regard the statement that happiness is the end as one of the numerous attempts which men have made to interpret the deliverances of their internal sense. I do not imagine the interpretation to be final and complete, and indeed it is too abstract and general to have very much meaning. But some meaning, no doubt, it has; and exactly what, may form the subject of much interesting discussion in detail, which belongs, however, rather to the question of the content of Good, than to that of the method of discovering it."

"The method!" replied Wilson, "but have you really indicated a method at all?"

"I have indicated," I replied "what I suppose to be the method of all science, namely, the interpretation of experience."

"But," he objected, "everything depends on the kind of interpretation."

"True," I admitted, "but long ago I did my best to prove that we could not learn anything about Good by the scientific method as you defined it. For that can tell us only about what is, not about what ought to be. At the same time, the recording and comparing and classifying of the deliverances of this internal sense, has a certain analogy to the procedure of science. At any rate, it might, I think, fairly be called a method, though a method difficult to apply, and one, above all, which only he can apply who has within himself the requisite experience. And in this respect the study of the Good resembles the study of the Beautiful."

"How do you mean?"

"Why," I said, "those who are conversant with the arts are well aware that there is such a thing as a true canon, though they do not profess to be in complete possession of it. They have a perception of the Beautiful, not ready-made and final, but tentative and in process of growth. This perception they cultivate by constant observation of beautiful works, some more and some less, according to their genius and opportunities; and thus they are always coming to see, though they never see perfectly, just as I said was the case in the matter of the Good."

"But," objected Parry, "what proof is there that there is any standard at all in such matters?"

"There is no proof," I replied, "except the perception itself; and that is sufficient proof to those who have it. And to some slight extent, no doubt, all men have it; only many do not care to develop it; and so, feeling in themselves that they have no standard of judgment in art, they suppose that all others are like themselves; and that there really is no standard and no knowledge possible in such matters. And it is the same with Good; if a man will not choose to cultivate his inner sense, and to train it to clear and ever clearer perception, he will either never believe that there is any knowledge of Good, or any meaning at all in the word; or else, since all men feel the need of an end for action, he will have recourse to a fixed dogma, taken up by accident and clung to with obstinate desperation, without any root in his true inner nature; and to him all discussion about Good will seem to be mere folly, since he will believe either that he possesses it already or that it cannot be possessed at all. Or if he ask after the method of discovering it, he will be unable to understand it, because he does not choose to develop the necessary experience; and so he will go through life for ever unconvinced, arguing often and angrily, but always with no result, while all the time the knowledge he denies is lying hidden within him, if only he had the patience and faith to seek it there. But without that, there is no possibility of convincing him; and it will be wiser altogether to leave him alone. This, whether you call it a method or no, is the only idea I can form as to the possibility of discovering what is Beautiful and Good."

There was silence for a few moments, and then Wilson said:

"Do you mean to imply, on your hypothesis, that we all are always seeking Good?"

"No," I said; "whatever I may think on that point, I have not committed myself. It is enough for my purpose if we admit that we have the faculty of seeking Good, supposing we choose to do so."

"And also the faculty of seeking Bad?"

"Possibly; I do not pronounce upon that."

"Well, anyhow, do you admit the existence of Bad?"

"Oh yes," I cried, "as much as you like; for it is bad, to my mind, that we should be in a difficult quest of Good, instead of in secure possession of it. And about the nature of that quest I make no facile assumption. I do not pretend that what I have called the growth of the soul from within is a smooth and easy process, a quiet unfolding of leafy green in a bright and windless air. If I recognize the delight of expansion, I recognize also the pain of repression—the thwarted desire, the unfulfilled hope, the passion vain and abortive. I do not say even whether or no, in this dim travail of the spirit, pleasure prevails over pain, evil over good. The most I would claim is to have suggested a meaning for our life in terms of Good; and my view, I half hoped, would have appealed in particular to you, because what I have offered is not an abstract formula, hard to interpret, hard to relate to the actual facts of life, but an attempt to suggest the significance of those facts themselves, to supply a key to the cryptogram we call experience. And in proportion as we really believed this view to be true, it would lead us not away from but into life, not shutting us up, as has been too much the bent of philosophy, like the homunculus of Goethe's 'Faust,' in the crystal phial of a set and rigid system, to ring our little chiming bell and flash our tiny light over the vast sea of experience, which all around us foams and floods, myriad-streaming, immense, and clearly seen, yet never felt, through that transparent barrier; but rather, like him when he broke the glass, made free of the illimitable main, to follow under the yellow moon the car of Galatea, her masque of nymphs and tritons, her gliding pomp of cymbals and conchs, away through tempest and calm, by night or day, companioned or alone, to the haunts of the far Cabeiri, and the home where the Mothers dwell."

As I concluded, I looked across at Audubon, to see if I had made any impression upon him. But he only smiled at me rather ironically and said, "Is that meant, may I ask, for an account of every-day experience?"

"Rather," I replied, "for an interpretation of it."

"It would need a great deal of interpretation," he said, "to make anything of the kind out of mine."

"No doubt," I said; "yet I am not without hope that the interpretation may be true; and that some day you may recognize it to be so yourself. Meantime, perhaps, I, who look on, see more of the game than you who play it; and surely in moments of leisure like this you will not refuse to listen to my poor attempt to read the riddle of the sphinx."

"Oh," he said, "I listen gladly enough, but as I would to a poem."

"And do you think," I replied, "that there is not more truth in poetry than in philosophy or science?"

But Wilson entered a vigorous protest, and for a time there was a babel of argument and declamation, from which no clear line of thought disengaged itself. Dennis, however, in his persistent way, had been revolving in his mind what I had said, and at the first opportunity he turned to me with the remark, "There's one point in your position that I can't understand. Do you mean to say that it is our seeking that determines the Good, or the Good that determines our seeking."

"Really," I said, "I don't know. I should say both are true. We, in the process of our seeking, affirm what we find to be good, and in that sense determine for ourselves what for us was previously indeterminate; but, on the other hand, our determination is not mere caprice; it is determination of Good, which we must therefore suppose somehow or other to 'be' before we discern it."

"But then, in what sense *is* it?"

"That is what it is so hard to say. Perhaps it is the law of our seeking, the creative and urging principle of the world, striving through us to realize itself, and recognized by us in that effort and strain."

"Then your hypothesis is that Good has to be brought about, even while you admit that in some sense it is?"

"Yes, it exists partially, and it ought to come to exist completely."

"Well now, that is exactly what seems to me absurd. If Good is at all it is eternal and complete."

"But then, I ask in my turn, in what sense *is* it?"

"In the only sense that anything really is. The rest is nothing but appearance."

"What we call Evil, you mean, is nothing but appearance."

"Yes."

"You think, in fact, with the poet, that 'all that is, is good'?"

"Yes," he replied, "all that really is."

"Ah!" I said, "but in that 'really' lies the crux of the matter. Take, for instance, a simple fact of our own experience—pain. Would you say, perhaps, that pain is good?"

"No," he replied, "not as it appears to us; but as it really is."

"As it really is to whom, or in whom?"

"To the Absolute, we will say; to God, if you like."

"Well, but what is the relation of the pain as it is in God to the pain that appears to us?"

"I don't pretend to know," he said, "but that is hardly the point. The point is, that it is only in connection with what is in God that the word Good has any real meaning. Appearance is neither good nor bad; it is simply not real."

"But," cried Audubon, interrupting in a kind of passion, "it is in appearance that we live and move and have our being. What is the use of saying that appearance is neither good nor bad, when we are feeling it as the one or the other every moment of our lives? And as to the Good that is in God, who knows or cares about it? What consolation is it to me when I am suffering from the toothache, to be told that God is enjoying the pain that tortures me? It is simply absurd to call God's Good good at all, unless it has some kind of relation to our Good."

"Well," said Dennis, "as to that, I can only say that, in my opinion, it is nothing but our weakness that leads us to take such a view. When I am really at my best, when my intellect and imagination are working freely, and the humours and passions of the flesh are laid to rest, I seem to see, with a kind of direct intuition, that the world, just as it is, is good, and that it is only the confusion and obscurity due to imperfect vision that makes us call it defective and wish to alter it for the better. When I perceive Truth at all, I perceive that it is also Good; and I cannot then distinguish between what is, and what ought to be."

"Really," cried Audubon, "really? Well, that I cannot understand."

"I hardly know how to make it clear," he replied, "unless it were by a concrete example. I find that when I think out any particular aspect of things, so far, that is to say, as I can think it out at all, all the parts and details fall into such perfect order and arrangement that it becomes impossible for me any longer to desire that anything should be other than it is. And that, even in the regions where at other times I am most prone to discover error and defect. You know, for instance, that I am something of an economist?"

"What are you not?" I said. "If you sin, it is not from lack of light!"

"Well," he continued, "there is, I suppose, no department of affairs which one is more inclined to criticise than this. And yet the more one investigates the more one discovers, even here, the harmony and necessity that pervade the whole universe. The ebb and flow of business from this trade or country to that, the rise and fall of wages, or of the rate of interest, the pouring of capital into or out of one industry or another, the varying relations of imports to exports, the periods of depression and recovery, and in close connection with all this the ever-changing conditions of the lives of countless workmen throughout the world, their well-being or ill-being, it may be their very life and death, together with the whole fate of future generations in health, capacity, opportunity, and the like,—all this complexus of things, so chaotic and unintelligible at the first view, so full, as we say, of iniquity, injustice, and the like, falls, as we penetrate further, into one vast and harmonious system, so inspiring to the imagination, so inevitable to the understanding, that our objections and cavillings, ethical, æsthetic, or what you will, simply vanish away at the clearer vision, or, if they persist, persist as mere irrelevant illusions; while we abandon ourselves to the contemplation of the whole, as of some world-symphony, whose dissonances, no less than its concords, are taken up and resolved in the irresistible march and progress, the ocean-flooding of the Whole. You will think," he continued, "that I am absurdly rhapsodical over what, after all, is matter prosaic enough; but what I wanted to suggest was that it is

Reality so conceived that appeals to me at once as Truth and as Good. This partial vision of mine in the economic sphere is a kind of type of the way in which I conceive the Absolute. I conceive Him to be a Being necessary and therefore perfect; a Being in face of whom our own incoherent and tentative criticisms, our complaints that this or that should, if only it could, be otherwise, our regrets, desires, aspirations, and the like, shew but as so many testimonies to our own essential imperfection, weaknesses to be surmounted, rather than signs of worth to stamp us, as we vainly boast, the elect of creation."

He finished; and I half expected that Leslie would intervene, since I saw, as I thought, many weak points in the position. But he kept silence, impressed, perhaps, by that idea of the Perfect and Eternal which has a natural home in the minds of the generous and the young. So I began myself rather tentatively:

"I think," I said, "I understand the position you wish to indicate; and so stated, in general terms, no doubt it is attractive. It is when we endeavour to work it out in detail that the difficulties appear. The position, as I understand it, is, that, from the point of view of the Absolute, what we call Evil and what we call Good simply have no existence. Good and Evil, in our sense, are mere appearances; and Good, in the absolute sense, is identical with the Absolute or with God?"

"Yes," he said, "that is my notion."

"And so, for example, to apply the idea in detail, in the region which you yourself selected, all that we regret, or hate, or fear in our social system—poverty, disease, starvation and the rest—is not really evil at all, does not in fact exist, but is merely what appears to us? There is, in fact, no social evil?"

"No," he replied, "in the sense I have explained there is none."

"Well then," I continued, "how is it with all our social and other ideals? Our desire to make our own lives and other people's lives happier? Our efforts to subdue nature, to conquer disease, to introduce order and harmony where there appears to be discord and confusion? How is it with those finer and less directly practical impulses by which you yourself are mainly pre-occupied—the quest of knowledge or of beauty for their own sake, the mere putting of ourselves into right relations with the universe, apart from any attempt to modify it? Are all these desires and activities mere illusions of ours, or worse than illusions, errors and even vices, impious misapprehensions of the absolutely Good, frivolous attempts to adapt the Perfect to our own imperfections?"

"No," he replied, "I would not put it so. Some meaning, I apprehend, there must be in time and change, and some meaning also in our efforts, though not, I believe, the meaning which we imagine. The divine life, as I conceive it, is a process; only a process that is somehow eternal, circular, so to speak, not rectilinear, much as Milton appears to imagine it when he describes the blessed spirits 'progressing the dateless and irrevoluble circle of eternity'; and of this eternal process our activity, which we suppose to be moving towards an end, is somehow or other an essential element. So that, in this way, it is necessary and right that we should strive after ideals; only, when we are thinking philosophically, we ought to make clear to ourselves that in truth the Ideal is eternally fulfilled, its fulfilment consisting precisely in that process which we are apt to regard as a mere means to its realization. This, as Hegel has it, is the 'cunning' of the Absolute Reason, which deludes us into the belief that there is a purpose to be attained, and by the help of that delusion preserves that energy of action which all the time is really itself the End."

I looked up at him as he finished, to see whether he was quite serious; and as he appeared to be so, and as Leslie still kept silence, I took up the argument as follows.

"I understand," I said, "in a sort of way what you mean; but still the same difficulty recurs which Audubon has already put forward. On your hypothesis there seems to be an impassable gulf between God's conception of Good and ours. To God, as it seems, the world is eternally good; and in its goodness is included that illusion by which it appears to us so bad, that we are continually employed in trying to make it better. The maintenance of this illusion is essential to the nature of the world; to us, evil always must appear. But, as we know by experience, the evil that *appears* is just as terrible and just as hateful as it would be if it really *were*. A toothache, as Audubon put it, is no less a pain to us because it is a pleasure to God. We cannot, if we would, adopt His point of view; and clearly it would be impious to try, since we should be endeavouring to defeat His ingenious plan to keep the world going by hoodwinking us. We therefore are chained and bound to the whirling wheel of appearance; to us what seems good is good, and what seems bad, bad; and your contention that all existence is somehow eternally good is for us simply irrelevant; it belongs to the point of view of God to which we have no access."

"Yes," cried Audubon, "and what a God to call God at all! Why not just as much the devil? What are we to think of the Being who is responsible for a world of whose economy our evil is not merely an accident, a mistake, but positively an essential, inseparable condition!"

"What, indeed!" exclaimed Leslie. "Call Him God, by all means, if you like, but such a God as Zeus was to Prometheus, omnipotent, indeed, and able to exact with infallible precision His daily and hourly toll of blood and tears, but powerless at least to chain the mind He has created free, or to exact allegiance and homage from spirits greater, though weaker, than Himself."

This was the sort of talk, I knew, that rather annoyed Dennis. I did not therefore, for the moment, leave him time to reply, but proceeded to a somewhat different point:

"Even putting aside," I said, "the moral character of God, as it appears in your scheme of the universe, must we not perhaps accuse Him of a slight lapse of intelligence? For, as I understand the matter, it was essential to the success of the Absolute's plan that we should never discover the deception that is being played upon us. But, it seems, we do discover it. Hegel, for example, by your own confession, has not only detected but exposed it. Well then, what is to be done? Do you suppose that we could, even if we would, continue to lend ourselves to the imposition? Must not our aims and purposes cease to have any interest for us, once we are clear that they are not true ends? And that which, according to the hypothesis, *is* the true end, the 'dateless and irrevoluble circle' of activity, that, surely, we at least cannot sanction or approve, seeing that it involves and perpetuates the very misery and pain whose destruction was our only motive for acting at all. For, whatever may be the case with God, we, you will surely admit, are forbidden by all that in us is highest and best, to approve or even to acquiesce in the deliberate perpetuation of a world of whose existence all that we call evil is an essential and eternal constituent. So that, as I said at first, it looks as if the Absolute Reason had not been, after all, quite as cunning as it thought, since it has allowed us to discover and expose the very imposition it had invented to cheat us into concurrence with its plans."

Dennis laughed a little at this; and then, "Well," he began, "between you, with your genial irony, and Audubon and Leslie with their heaven-defying rhetoric, I scarcely know whether I stand on my head or my heels. But, the fact is, I think I made a slip in stating my view; or perhaps there was really a latent contradiction in my mind. At any rate, what I believe, whether or no I can believe it consistently, is that it is possible for us, so to speak, to take God's point of view; so that the evil against which we rebel we may come at last to acquiesce in, as seen from the higher point of view. And, seriously, don't you think it is conceivable that that may be, after all, the true meaning of the discipline of life?"

"I cannot tell," I said, "perhaps it may. But, meantime, allow me to press home the importance of your admission. For, as you say, there is at least one of our aims which has a real significance, namely, that of reaching the point of view of God. But this is something that lies in the future, something to be brought about. And so, on your own hypothesis, Good, after all, would not be that which eternally exists, but something which has to be realized in time—namely, a change of mind on the part of all rational beings, whereby they view the world no longer in a partial imperfect way, but, in Spinoza's phrase, '*sub specie æternitatis.*'"

"No," he said, "I cannot admit that that is an end for the Absolute, though I admit it is an end for us. The Absolute, somehow or other, is eternally perfect and good; and this eternal perfection and goodness are unaffected by any change that may take place in our minds."

"Well," I said, "I must leave it to the Absolute and yourself to settle how that can possibly be. Meantime, I am content with your admission that, for us, at least, there is an end and a Good lying before us to be realized in the future. For that, as I understand, you do admit. In your own life, for example, even if you aim at nothing else, or at nothing else which you wholly approve, yet you do aim, at least, with your whole nature at this—to attain a view of the world as it may be conceived in its essence to be, not merely as it appears to us."

"Yes," he said, "I admit that is my aim."

"That aim, then, is your Good?"

"I suppose so."

"And it is something, as I said, that lies in the future? For you do not, I suppose, count yourself to have attained, or at least to have attained as perfectly as you hope to?"

He agreed again.

"Well then," I continued, "what may be the relation of this Good of yours, awaiting realization in the future, to that eternal Good of God in which you also believe, we will reserve, with your permission, for some future inquiry. It is enough for our present purpose that even you, who assert the eternal perfection of the world, do nevertheless at the same time admit a future Good; and much more do other men admit it, who have no idea that the world is perfect at all. So that we may, I think, safely suppose it to be generally agreed that the Good is something to be realized in the future, so far, at any rate as it concerns us—and, for my part, I have no desire to go farther than that."

"Well," he said, "I am content for the present to leave the matter so. But I reserve the right to go back upon the argument."

"Of course!" I replied, "for it is not, I hope, an argument, but a discussion; and a discussion not for victory but for truth. Meantime, then, let us take as a hypothesis that Good is something to be brought about; and let us consider next the other point that is included in your position. According to you, as I understand, what requires to be brought about, if ever Good is to be realized, is not any change in the actual stuff, so to speak, of the world, in the structure, as it were, of our experience, but only a change in our attitude towards all this—a change in the subject, as they say, and not in the object. Our aim should be not to abolish what we call evil, by successive modifications of physical and social conditions, but rather, all these remaining essentially the same, to come to see that what appears to be evil is not really so."

"Yes," he said, "that is the view I would suggest."

"So that, for example, though we might still experience a toothache, we should no longer regard it as an evil; and so with all the host of things we are in the habit of calling bad: they would continue unchanged 'in themselves,' as you Hegelians say, only to us they would appear no longer bad, but good?"

"Yes; as I said at first, all reality is good, and all Evil, so-called, is merely illusion."

I was about to reply when I was forestalled by Bartlett. For some time past the discussion had been left pretty much to Dennis and myself, with an occasional incursion from Audubon and Leslie. Ellis had gone indoors; Parry and Wilson were talking together about something else; and Bartlett appeared to be still absorbed in the *Chronicle.* I noticed, however, that for the last few moments he had been getting restless, and I suspected that he was listening, behind his newspaper, to what we were saying. I was not therefore altogether surprised when, upon Dennis' last remark, he suddenly broke into our debate with the exclamation:

"Would it be 'in order' to introduce a concrete example? There is a curiously apt one here in the *Chronicle.*"

And upon our assenting, he read us a long extract about phosphorus-poisoning, the details of which I now forget, but at any rate it brought before us, very vividly, a tale of cruel suffering and oppression.

"Now," he said, as he finished, "is that, may I ask, the kind of thing that it amuses you to call mere illusion?"

"Yes," replied Dennis stoutly, "that will do very well for an example."

"Well," he rejoined, "I do not propose to dispute about words; but for my own part I should have thought that, if anything is real, that is; and so, I think, you would find it, if you yourself were the sufferer."

"But," objected Dennis, "do you think that it is in the moment of suffering that one is most competent to judge about the reality of pain?"

"Certainly, for it is only in the moment of suffering that one really knows what it is that one is judging about."

"I am not sure about that. I doubt whether it is true that experience involves knowledge and *vice versa.* It is, indeed, to my mind, part of the irony of life, that we know so much which we can never experience, and experience so much which we can never know."

"I don't follow that," said Bartlett, "but of one

thing I am sure, that you will never get rid of evil by calling it illusion."

"No," Dennis conceded, "you will never of course get rid of it, in the sense you mean, by that, or indeed, in my opinion, by any other means. But we were discussing not what we are to do with evil, but how we are to conceive it."

"But," he objected, "if you begin by conceiving it as illusion, you will never do anything with it at all."

"Perhaps not, but I am not sure that that is my business."

"At any rate, Dennis," I interposed, "you will, I expect, admit, that for us, while we live in the region of what you call 'Appearance,' Evil is at least as pressing and as obvious as Good."

"Yes," he said, "I am ready to admit that."

"And," I continued, "for my part I agree with Bartlett and with Leslie, that it is Appearance with which we are concerned. What I have been contending for throughout, is that in the world in which we live (whether we are to call it Reality or Appearance), Evil and Good are the really dominating facts; and that we cannot dismiss them from our consideration either on the ground that we know nothing of them (as Ellis was inclined to maintain) or on the ground that we know all about them (as Parry and Wilson seemed to think). On the contrary, it is, I believe, our main business to find out about them; and that we can find out about them is with me an article of faith, and so, I believe, it is with most people, whether or no they are aware of it or are ready to admit it."

Dennis was preparing to reply, when Ellis re-appeared to summon us to lunch. We followed him in gladly enough, for it was past our usual hour and we were hungry; and the conversation naturally taking a lighter turn, I have nothing further to record until we reassembled in the afternoon.

BOOK II.

WHEN we reassembled for coffee on the loggia after lunch, I did not suppose we should continue the morning's discussion. The conversation had been turning mostly on climbing, and other such topics, and finally had died away into a long silence, which, for my own part, I felt no particular inclination to break. We had let down an awning to shelter us from the sun, where it began to shine in upon us, so that it was still cool and pleasant where we sat; and so delightful did I feel the situation to be, that I was almost vexed to be challenged to renew our interrupted debate. The challenge, rather to my surprise, came from Audubon, who suddenly said to me, *à propos* of nothing, in a tone at once ironic and genial:

"Well, I thought you talked very well this morning."

"Really!" I rejoined, "I imagined you were thinking it all great nonsense."

"So no doubt it was," he replied; "still, it amused me to hear you."

"I am glad of that, at any rate; I was afraid perhaps you were bored."

"Not at all. Of course, I couldn't fail to see that you weren't arriving anywhere. But that I never expected. In fact, what amuses me most about you is, the way in which you continue to hope that you're going to get at some result."

"But didn't we?"

"I don't see that you did. You showed, or tried to show, that we must believe in Good; but you made no attempt to discover what Good is."

"No," I admitted; "that, of course, is much more difficult."

"Exactly; but it is the only point of importance."

"Well," I said, "perhaps if we were to try, we should find that we can come to some agreement even about that."

"I don't believe it."

"But why not?"

"Because people are so radically different, that there is no common ground to build upon."

"But is the difference really so radical as all that?"

"Yes," he said, "I think so. At any rate, the proof of the pudding is in the eating, and I make you an offer. Here are eight of us, all Englishmen, all contemporaries, all brought up more or less in the same way. And I venture to say that, if you will raise the question, you won't find, even among ourselves, with all the chances in your favour, any substantial agreement about what we think good."

This direct challenge was rather alarming. I didn't feel that I could refuse to take it up, but I was anxious to guard myself against the consequences of failure. So I began, with some hesitation, "You must remember that I have never maintained that at any given moment any given set of people will be found to be in agreement on all points. All I ventured to suggest was, that instead of our all being made, as you contend, radically different, we have, underneath our differences, a common nature, capable of judging, and judging truly, about Good, though only on the basis of actual experience of Good. And on this view I shall, of course, expect to find differences of opinion, corresponding to differences of experience, even among people as much alike as ourselves; only I shall not expect the differences to be finally irreconcilable, but that we shall be able to supplement and elucidate one another's conclusions by bringing to bear each his own experience upon that of the rest."

"Well," he said, "we shall see. I have invited you to make the experiment."

"I am willing," I replied, "if it is agreeable to the others. Only I must ask you to understand from the beginning precisely what it is I am trying to do. I shall be merely describing to you what I have been able to perceive, with such experience as I have had, in this difficult matter; and you will judge, all of you, whether or no, and to what extent, your perceptions coincide with mine, the object being simply to clear up these perceptions of ours, if we can; to define somehow, as it were, what we have seen, in the hope of coming to see something more."

They agreed to take me on my own terms, and I was about to begin, when, happening to catch Dennis' eye, I suddenly felt discouraged. "After all," I said, "I doubt whether it's much use my making the attempt."

"Why, what's the matter?"

"Nothing," I said. "At least—well, I may as well confess it, though it seems like giving away my whole case. The fact is, that there are certain quite fundamental points in this connection on which Dennis and I have never been able to agree; and although I believe we should in time come to understand one another, I doubt whether we can do so here and now. At any rate, he doesn't look at all as if he meant to make it easy for me; and if I cannot carry him along with me, I suppose I may as well give up at once."

"Oh," said Audubon, "if that is all, I will make a concession. We will leave Dennis out of the reckoning. It shall be enough if you can persuade the rest of us."

"But," I urged, "I doubt, even so, whether Dennis will ever allow me to get to the end. You see, he never lets things pass if he doesn't happen to agree."

"Oh," cried Ellis, "it's all right. We will keep him in order."

Dennis laughed. "You're disposing of me," he said, "in a very easy manner. But perhaps I had better go away altogether; for, if I stay, I certainly cannot pledge myself not to interrupt."

"No," I said, "that seems hardly fair. What I propose is, that we should both try to be as conciliatory as we can. And then, by the process of 'give and take,' I shall perhaps slip past you without any really scandalous concession on either side."

"Well," he said, "you can try."

So, after casting about in my mind, I began, with some hesitation, as follows:

"The first thing, then, that I want to say is this: Good, as it seems to me, necessarily involves some form of conscious activity."

As I had expected, Dennis interrupted me at once.

"I don't see that at all," he said. "Consciousness may have nothing to do with it."

"Perhaps, indeed, it may not," I replied, with all the suavity I could command. "I should rather have said that I, as a matter of fact, can form no idea of Good except in connection with consciousness."

"Can you not?" he exclaimed, "but I can! If a thing is good it's good, so it appears to me, whether or no there is any consciousness of it."

"But," I said, "I, you see, myself, have no experience of anything existing apart from consciousness, so it is difficult for me to know whether such a thing would be good or no. But you, perhaps, are differently constituted."

"Not in that point," he replied. "I admit, of course, that there is no experience without consciousness. But we can surely conceive that of which we have no experience? And I should have thought it was clear that Good, like Truth, *is*, whether or no anyone is aware of it. Or would you say that $2 + 2 = 4$ is only true when someone is thinking of it?"

"As to that," I replied, "I would rather not say anything about it just now. On the logical point you may be right; but that, I think, need not at present detain us, because what I am trying to get at, for the moment, is something rather different. I will put it like this: Good, if it is to be conceived as an object of human action, must be conceived, must it not, as an object of consciousness? For otherwise do you think we should trouble to pursue it?"

"I don't know," he said, "whether we should; but perhaps we ought to."

"But," I urged, "do you really think we ought? Do you think, to take an example, that it could be a possible or a right aim for an artist, say, to be perpetually producing, in a state of complete unconsciousness, works which on completion should be immediately hermetically sealed and buried for all eternity at the bottom of the sea? Do you think that he could or ought to consider such production as a Good? And so with all the works of man. Do we, and really ought we to, do anything except with some reference to consciousness?"

"I don't know whether we do," he replied, "but I think it quite possible that we ought."

"Well," I said, "we shall not, I suppose, just now, come to a closer agreement. But is there anyone else who shares your view? for, if not, I will, with your permission, go on to the next point."

None spoke, and Dennis made no further opposition. So, after a pause, I proceeded as follows: "I shall assume, then, that Good, in the sense in which I am conceiving it, as an end of human action, involves some kind of conscious activity. And the next question would seem to be, activity of whom?"

"That, at any rate," said Leslie, "appears to be simple enough. It must be an activity of some person or persons."

"Once more," murmured Dennis, "I protest."

But this time I ventured to ignore him, and merely said, in answer to Leslie, "The question, then, will be, what persons?"

"Why," he replied, "ourselves, I suppose!"

"What do you say, Parry?" I asked.

"I don't quite understand," he replied, "the kind of way you put your questions. But my own idea has always been, what I suppose is most people's now, that the Good we are working for is that of some future generation."

At this Leslie made some inarticulate interjection, which I thought it better to ignore. And, answering Parry, I said, "Suppose, then, we were to make a beginning by examining your hypothesis."

"By all means," he said, "though I should have thought we should all have accepted it—unless, perhaps, it were Dennis."

"I most certainly don't!" cried Leslie.

"Nor I," added Audubon.

"Oh you!" cried Parry, "you accept nothing!"

"True"; he replied, "my motto is 'j'attends.'"

"Well," I resumed, "let us follow the argument and see where it leads us. The hypothesis is, that Good involves some state of activity of some generation indefinitely remote. Is not that so, Parry?"

"Yes," he said, "and one can more or less define what the state of activity, as you call it, will be."

"Of course," interposed Ellis, "it will be one of heterogeneous, co-ordinate, coherent——"

"That," I interrupted, "is not at present the question. The question is merely as to the location of Good. According to Parry, it is located in this particular remote generation, and, I suppose, in those that follow it. But now, what about all the other generations, from the beginning of the world onward? Good, it would seem, can have no meaning for them, since it is the special privilege of those who come after them."

"Oh, yes, it has!" he replied, "for it is their business to bring it about, not indeed for themselves, but for their successors."

"But," cried Leslie, "what an absurd idea! Countless myriads of men and women are born upon the earth, live through their complex lives of action and suffering, pleasure and pain, hopes, fears, satisfactions, aspirations, and the like, pursuing what they call Good, and avoiding what they call Bad, under the naïf impression that there is Good and Bad for them—and yet the significance of all this is not really for themselves at all, but for some quite other people who will have the luck to be born in the remote future, and for whose sake alone their fellow-creatures, from the very beginning of time, have been brought into being like so many lifeless tools, to be used up and laid aside, when done with, on the black infinite ash-heap of the dead."

"Oh, come!" said Parry, "you exaggerate! These tools, as you call them, have a good enough time. It does not follow, because the final Good lies in the future, that the present has no Good at all. It has just as much Good as people can get out of it."

"But then," said Leslie, "in that case it is this Good of their own with which each generation is really concerned. So far as they do get Good at all they get it as an activity in themselves."

"Certainly," said Ellis; "and for my own part, I am sick of that cant of living for future generations. Let us, at least, live for ourselves, whether we live well or badly."

"Well," replied Parry, rather stiffly, "of course every one has his own ideas. But I confess that, for my own part, the men I admire are those who have sacrificed themselves for the future."

"But, Parry," I interposed, "let us get clear about this; and with a view to clearness let us take our own case. We, as I understand you, have to keep in view a double Good: first, a Good for ourselves, which is not indeed the perfect Good (for that is reserved for a future generation), but still is something Good as far as it goes—whether it be a certain degree of happiness, or however else we may have to define it; and as to this Good, there appears to be no difficulty, for we who pursue it are also the people who get it. That is so, is it not?"

He agreed.

"But now," I continued, "we come to the point of dispute. For besides this Good of our own, we have also, according to the theory, to consider a Good in which we have no share, that of those who are to be born in some indefinite future. And to this remote and alien Good we have even, on occasion, to sacrifice our own."

"Certainly," he said, "all good citizens will think so."

"I believe," I admitted, "that they will. And yet, how strange it seems! For consider it in this way. Imagine that the successive generations can somehow be viewed as contemporaneous—being projected, as it were, from the plane of time into that of space."

"It's rather hard," he said, "to imagine that."

"Well, but try, for the sake of argument; and consider what we shall have. We shall have a society divided into two classes, composed, the one of all the generations who, if they followed one another in time, would precede the first millenarian one; the other of all the millenarian generations themselves. And of these two classes the first would be perpetually engaged in working for the second, sacrificing to it, if need be, on occasion, all its own Good, but without any hope or prospect of ever entering itself into that other Good which is the monopoly of the other class, but to the production of which its own efforts are directed. What should we say of such a society? Should we not say that it was founded on injustice and inequality, and all those other phrases with which we are wont to denounce a system of serfdom or slavery?"

"But," he objected, "your projection of time into space has falsified the whole situation. For in fact the millenarian generation would not come into being until the others had ceased to be; and therefore the latter would not be being sacrificed to it."

"No," I said, "but they would have been sacrificed; and surely it comes to the same thing?"

"I am not sure," he replied, "and anyhow, I don't think sacrifice is the right word. In a society every man's interest is in the Whole; and when he works for the Whole he is also working for himself."

"No doubt that is true," I replied, "in a society properly constituted, but I question whether it would be true in such a society as I have described. And then there is a further difficulty—and here, I confess, my projection of time into space really does falsify the issue; for in the succession of generations in time, where *is* the Whole? Each generation comes into being, passes, and disappears; but how, or in what, are they summed up?"

"Why," he said, "in a sense they are all summed up in the last generation."

"But in what sense? Do you mean that their consciousness somehow persists into it, so that they actually enjoy its Good?"

"Of course not," he said, "but I mean that it was conditioned by them, and is the result of their labour and activities."

"In that sense," I replied, "you might say that the oysters I eat are summed up in me. But it would be a poor consolation to the oysters!"

"Well," he rejoined, "whatever you may say, I still think it right that each generation should sacrifice itself (as you call it) for the next. And so, I believe, would you, when it came to the point. At any rate, I have often heard you inveigh against the shortsightedness of modern politicians, and their unwillingness to run great risks and undertake great labours for the future."

"Quite true," I said, "that is the view I take. But I was trying to see how the view could be justified. For it seems to me, I confess, that we can only be expected to labour for what is, in some sense or other, our own Good; and I do not see how the Good of future generations, in your way of putting it, is also ours."

"But," he said, "we have an instinct that it is."

"I believe we have," I replied, "but the question would be, what that instinct really means. Somehow or other, I think it must mean, as you yourself suggested, that our Good is the Good of the Whole. Only the difficulty is to see how there is a Whole at all."

"Well," he said, "perhaps there is no Whole. What then?"

"Why, then," I replied, "how can we justify an instinct which bids us labour and sacrifice ourselves for a Good, which, on this hypothesis, has no significance for us, but only for other people."

"Perhaps," he said, "we cannot justify it, but I am sure we ought to obey it; and, indeed, I believe we cannot do otherwise. Even taking the view that the order of the world is altogether unjust, as I admit it would be on the view we are considering, yet, since we cannot remedy the injustice, we are bound at least to make the best of it; and the best we can do is to prepare the Good for those who come after us, even though we can never enter into it ourselves."

"I am not so sure about that," Ellis interrupted, "I think the best we can do is to try and realize Good for ourselves—as much as we can get, even if we admit that this is but little. For we do at least know, or may hope to discover, what Good for ourselves is; whereas Good for other people is far more hypothetical."

"But, surely," he objected, "that would lead to action we cannot approve—to a sacrifice of all larger Goods to our own pleasure of the moment. We should breed, for example, without any regard to the future efficacy of the race——"

"That," interrupted Ellis, "we do as it is."

"Yes, but we don't justify it—those of us, at least, who think. And, again, we should squander on immediate gratifications wealth which ought to be stored up against the future. And so on, and so on; it is not necessary to multiply examples."

"But," I objected, "we should only do these things if we thought that kind of short-sighted activity to be good; but, as a matter of fact, we do not, we who object to it. And that is because, as I hinted before, our idea of even our own Good is that of an activity in and for the Whole, and not merely in and for ourselves. And, whether it is reasonable or no, we cannot help extending the idea of the Whole, so as to include future generations. But, as it seems to me, the real meaning and justification of our action is not merely that we are seeking the Good of future generations but that we are endeavouring to realize our own Good, which consists in some such form of activity. So that really, as was suggested at the beginning, Good will be a kind of activity in ourselves, even though that activity be directed towards ends in which we do not expect to share."

At this point, Dennis, who had been struggling to speak, broke in at last, in spite of Ellis's efforts to restrain him.

"Why do you keep saying '*Our* Good'?" he

cried. "Why do you not say *the* Good? I can't understand this talk of me and thee, our Good, and their Good, as if there were as many Goods as there are people."

"Well," I said, "the distinction, after all, was introduced by Parry, who said that we ought to aim at the Good of a future generation. Still, I admit that I was getting a little unhappy myself at the kind of language into which I was betrayed. But what I want to say is this: So far as it is true at all that it is good to labour for future generations, goodness consists in the activity of so labouring, as much, at least, as in the result produced in those for whose sake the labour is. That, at least, is the only way in which I can find the position reasonable at all."

"I don't see it," said Parry, and was preparing to re-state his position, when Wilson suddenly intervened with a new train of thought.

"The fact is," he said, "you have begun altogether at the wrong end."

"I daresay," I said, "I can't find the end; it's all such a coil."

"Well," he said, "this is where I believe the trouble came in. You started with the idea that the Good must be good for individuals; and that was sure to land you in confusion."

"What then is your idea?" I asked.

"Why," he said, "as you might expect from a biologist, I regard everything from the point of view of the species."

At this I saw Ellis sit up and prepare for an encounter.

"Nature," continued Wilson, "has always in view the Whole not the Part, the species not the individual. And this law, which is true of the whole creation, is thrown into special relief in the case of man, because there the interest of the species is embodied in a particular form—the Society or the State—and may be clearly envisaged, as a thing apart, towards the maintenance of which conscious efforts may be directed."

"And this, which is the end of Nature, according to you, is also the Good?"

"Naturally."

"Well," I said, "I will not recapitulate here the objections I have already urged against the view that the course of Nature determines the content of the Good. For, quite apart from that, it is a view which many people hold—and one which was held long before there was a science of biology—that the community is the end, and the individual only the means."

"But," he said, "biology has given a new basis and a new colour to the view."

"I don't know about that," cried Ellis, unable any longer to restrain himself, "but I am sure it has given us a new kind of language. In the old days, when Wilson's opinion was represented by Plato, men were still men, and were spoken of as such, however much they might be subordinated to the community. But now!—why, if you open one of these sociological books, mostly, I am bound to say, in German, 'Entwurf einer Sozialanthropologie,' 'Versuch einer anthropologischen Darstellung der menschlichen Gesellschaft vom

Sozial-biologischen Standpunkt aus,' and the like—you will hardly be able to realize that you are dealing with human beings at all. I have seen an unmarried woman called a 'female non-childbearing human.' And at the worst, men actually cease to be even animals; they become mere numbers; they are calculated by the theory of combinations; they are masses, averages, classes, curves, anything but men! For every million of the population, it has been solemnly estimated, there will be one genius, one imbecile, 256,791 individuals just above the mean, 256,791 just below it! Observe, 256,791! Not, as one might have been tempted to believe, 256,790! What a saving grace in that odd unit! And this is the kind of thing that is revolutionizing history and politics! No more great men, no more heroic actions, no more inspirations, passions, and ideals! Nothing but calculations of the chances that A will meet and breed out of B! Nothing but analysis of the mechanism of survival! Nothing but——"

"My dear Ellis," interrupted Wilson, "you appear to me to be digressing."

"Digressing!" he cried. "Would that I could digress out of this world altogether! Would that I could digress to a planet where they have no arithmetic! Where a man could be a man, not a figure in an addition sum, a unit in an average, an individual in a species——"

"Where," exclaimed Audubon, taking him up, "a man could be himself, as I have often said, 'imperial, plain, and true.'"

There was a chorus of protestation at the too

familiar quotation; and for a time I was unable to lay hold of the broken thread of the argument. But at last I got a hearing for the question I was anxious to address to Wilson.

"You say," I began, "that by Good we mean the Good of the community?"

"I say," he replied, "that that is what we ought to mean."

"But in what sense do you understand the word community?"

"In the sense of that organization of individuals which represents, so to speak, the species."

"How represents?"

"In the sense that it is its function to maintain and perfect the species."

"But is that the function of the community?"

"If it is not, it ought to be; and to a great extent it is. If you look at the social mechanism, not with the eyes of a mere historian, who usually sees nothing, but with those of a biologist and man of science, intent upon essentials, you will find that it is nothing but an elaborate apparatus of selection, natural or artificial, as you like to call it. First, there is the struggle of races, which may be traced not only in war and conquest, but more insidiously under the guise of peace, so that, for example, at this day you may witness throughout Europe the gradual extinction of the long-headed fair by the round-headed dark stock. Then there is the struggle of nation with nation, resulting in the gradual elimination of the weaker—that, of course, is obvious enough; but what is not always so clearly seen is the not less certain fact, that within the limits of each society the same process is everywhere at work. To pass over the economic struggle for existence, of which we are perhaps sufficiently aware, what else is our system of examinations but a mechanism of selection, whereby it is determined that certain persons only shall have access to certain professions? What else is the convention whereby marriages are confined to people of the same class, thus securing the perpetuation of certain types, and especially of the better-gifted and better-disposed? Turn where we may we find the same phenomenon. Society is a machine for sifting out the various elements of the race, combining the like, disparting the unlike, bringing some to the top, others to the bottom, preserving these, eliminating those, indifferent to the fate, good or bad, of the individuals it controls, but envisaging always the well-being of the Whole."

"But," I objected, "is it so certain that it is well-being that is kept in view? Do you not recognize a process of deterioration as well as of improvement? You mentioned, for instance, that the long-headed fair race, is giving place to what I understand is regarded as an inferior type."

"No doubt," he admitted, "there are periods of decline. Still, on the whole, the movement is an upward one."

"Well," I replied, "that, after all, is not the question we are at present discussing. Your main point is, that when we speak of Good we mean, or should mean, the Good, not of the individual, but of the species. But what, I should like to know, is the species? Is it somehow an entity, or being, that it has a Good?"

"No," he replied, "it is merely, of course, a general name for the individuals; only for all the individuals taken together, not one by one or in groups."

"The Good of the species, then, is the Good of all the individuals taken together."

"Yes."

"But," I said, "how can that be? It is good for the species, according to you, that certain individuals should be eliminated, or should sink to the bottom, or whatever else their fate may be. But is that also good for the individual in question?"

"I don't know about that," he replied, "and I don't see that it matters. I only say that it is good for the species."

"But they are part of the species; so that if it is good for the species it is good for them."

"No! for the Good of the species consists in the selection of the best individuals. It is indifferent to all the rest."

"Then by the Good of the species you mean the good of the selected individuals?"

"Not exactly; I mean it is good that those individuals should be selected."

"But good for whom, if not for them? For the individuals who are eliminated? Or for you who look on? Or perhaps, for God?"

"God! No! I mean good, simply good."

"I'm afraid I don't understand," I said. "Does Good then hang, as it were, in the air, being Good for nobody at all?"

"Well, if you like, we will say it is good for Nature."

"But is Nature, then, a conscious being?"

"I don't say that."

"I am very sorry," I said, "but really I cannot understand you. If you reject God, I see only two alternatives remaining. Either the Good you speak of is that of all the individuals of the species taken together, or it is that of the best individuals; and in either case I seem to see difficulties."

"What difficulties?" asked Parry. For Wilson did not speak.

"Why," I said, "taking the first alternative, I do not see how it can be good for the inferior individuals to be degraded or eliminated. I should have thought, if there were any Good for them, it would consist in their being made better."

"I don't see that," objected Dennis; "it might be the best possible thing, for them, to be eliminated."

"But in that case," I said, "the best possible thing would be absence of Bad, not Good. And so far as we could talk of Good at all, we could not apply it to them?"

"Perhaps not."

"Well then, in that case we have to fall back upon the other alternative, and say that by the Good of the species we mean that of the ultimately selected individuals."

"Well, what then?"

"Why, then, we return, do we not, to the position of Parry, that the Good is that of some particular generation? And there, too, we were met by difficulties. So that altogether I do not really see what meaning to attach to Wilson's conception."

"There is no meaning to be attached to it!" cried Ellis. "The species is a mere screen invented to conceal the massacre of individuals. I'm sick of these biologico-sociologico-anthropologico-historico treatises, with their talk of races, of nations, of classes, never of men! their prate about laws as if they were the real entities, and the people who are supposed to be subject to them mere indifferent particles of stuff! their analysis of the perfection with which the machine works, its combinations, differentiations, subordinations, co-ordinations, and all the other abominations of desolations standing where they ought not, as depressing to the mind as they are cacophonous to the ear! and, worst of all, their impudent demand that we should admire the diabolical process! Admire! As though we should be asked to admire the beauty of the rack and the thumbscrew!"

"It's a matter of taste, no doubt," said Wilson, "but in me the spectacle of natural law does awaken feelings of admiration."

"In me," replied Ellis, "it awakens, just as often, feelings of disgust, and especially when its theatre is human life."

"At any rate, whether you admire it or not, the spectacle is there."

"No doubt, if you choose to look at it; but why should you? It's not a good drama; it isn't up to date; it has no first-hand knowledge, nor original vision of life. It simply ignores all the important facts."

"Which do you call the important facts?"

"Why, of course, the emotions; the hopes, fears, aspirations, sympathies and the rest! There's more valuable information contained in even an inferior novel that in all the sociological treatises that ever have been or will be written."

"Oh, come!" cried Parry.

"I assure you," replied Ellis, "I am serious. Take, for example, these unfortunate creatures who are in process of elimination. To the sociologist their elimination is their only *raison d'être.* He cancels them out with the same delight as if they were figures in a complex fraction. But pick up any novel dealing with the life of the slums, and you find that these figures are really composed of innumerable individual units, existing each for himself, and each his own sufficient justification, each a sacred book comprising its own unique secret, a master-piece of the divine tragedian, a universe self-moved and self-contained, a centre of infinity, a mirror of totality, in a word, a human soul."

"All that I altogether deny," said Wilson, "but, even if it were true, it would not affect the sociological laws."

"I don't say it would. I only say that the sociological laws are as unimportant, if possible, as the law of gravitation."

"Which," replied Wilson, "may be regarded as a *reductio ad absurdum* of your view."

"Anyhow," I interposed, "we are digressing from our point. What I really want to know is whether Wilson has any more light to throw on my difficulties with regard to his notion of the species."

"I have nothing more to say," he replied, "than I have said already."

"But I have!" cried Dennis, "and something very

much to the point. You see now the absurdities into which you are led by the position you insisted on assuming, that Good involves conscious activity. If it does, as you rightly inquired (though with a suicidal audacity), conscious activity in whom? And to that question, of course, you can find no answer."

"And yet," I said, endeavouring to turn the tables upon him, "I have known you to maintain yourself that Good not merely involves, but is, a conscious activity; only an activity in or of God."

"Rather," he replied, "that it *is* God. But I don't really know whether we ought to call God a conscious activity. Whatever He or It be, is something that transcends our imagination. Only the things we call good are somehow reflexes of God; and we have to accept them as such without further inquiry. At any rate, we have no right to endeavour, as you keep doing, to locate Good in some individual persons."

"Well," I said, "here we come again to a fundamental difference of view. All the Good of which I am aware as actually existing is associated, somehow or other, with personal consciousness. I am willing to admit, for the sake of argument, that the ultimate Good, if ever we come to know it, might, perhaps, not be so associated. But of that, as yet, I know nothing; you, perhaps, are more fortunate. And if you can give us an account of Good, I mean, of course, of its content, which shall represent it intelligibly to us as independent of any consciousness like our own, I am quite ready to relinquish the argument to you."

"I don't know," he replied, "that I can represent it to you in a way that you would admit to be intelligible. I don't profess to have had what you call 'experience' of it."

"Well, then," said Ellis, "what's the good of talking?"

"What, indeed!" I echoed, in some despondency. For I began to feel it was impossible to carry on the conversation. But at this point, to my great relief, Bartlett came to the rescue, not indeed with a solution of the difficulty in which we were involved, but with a diversion of which I was only too glad to take advantage.

"It seems to me," he said, "that you are getting off the track! Whatever the ultimate Good may be, what we really want to know, is the kind of thing we can conceive to be good for people like ourselves. And I thought that was what you were going to discuss."

"So I was," I said, "if Dennis would have let me."

"I will let you, by all means," Dennis interposed, "so long as it is quite understood that everything you say has nothing to do with the real subject."

"Very well," said Bartlett, "that's understood. And now let's get along, on the basis of you and me and the man in the street. What are we trying to get, when we try to get Good? That I take it is the real question."

"And I can only answer," I said, "as I did before, that we are trying to get some state of conscious experience, to enter into some activity."

Very well, then, what activity?" he inquired,

catching me up sharp, as if he were afraid of Dennis interposing again.

"What activity!" cried Ellis, "why all and every one as much as another, and the more the merrier."

"What!" I exclaimed, rather taken aback, "all at once do you mean? whether they be good or whether they be bad, all alike indifferently?"

"There are no bad activities," he replied, "none bad essentially in themselves. Their goodness and badness depends on the way in which they are interchanged or combined. Any pursuit or occupation palls in time if it is followed exclusively; but all may be delightful in the just measure and proportion. We are complex creatures, and we ought to employ all our faculties alike, never one alone at the cost of all the others."

"That may be sound enough," I said, "but will you not describe more in detail the kind of life which you consider to be good?"

"How can I?" he replied. "It is like trying to sum infinity! The most I can do is to hint and rhapsodize."

"Hint away, then!" cried Parry; "rhapsodize away! we're all listening."

"Well, then," he said, "my ideal of the good life would be to move in a cycle of ever-changing activity, tasting to the full the peculiar flavour of each new phase in the shock of its contrast with that of all the rest. To pass, let us say, from the city with all its bustle, smoke, and din, its press of business, gaiety, and crime, straight away, without word or warning, breaking all engagements, to the farthest and loneliest corner of the world. To hunt or fish for weeks and months in strange wild places, camping out among strange beasts and birds, lost in pathless forests, or wandering over silent plains. Then, suddenly, back in the crowd, to feel the press of business, to make or lose millions in a week, to adventure, compete, and win; but always, at the moment when this might pall, with a haven of rest in view, an ancient English mansion, stately, formal, and august, islanded, over its sunken fence, by acres of buttercups. There to study, perhaps to write, perhaps to experiment, dreaming in my garden at night of new discoveries, to revolutionize science and bring the world of commerce to my feet. Then, before I have time to tire, to be off on my travels again, washing gold in Klondike, trading for furs in Siberia, fighting in Madagascar, in Cuba, or in Crete, or smoking hasheesh in tents with Persian mystics. To make my end action itself, not anything action may gain, choosing not to pursue the Good for fear I should let slip Goods, but, in my pursuit of Goods, attaining the only Good I can conceive—a full and harmonious exercise of all my faculties and powers."

On hearing him speak thus I felt, I confess, such a warmth of sympathy that I hesitated to attempt an answer. But Leslie, who was young enough still to live mainly in ideas, broke in with his usual zeal and passion.

"But," he said, "all this activity of which you speak is no more good than it is bad; every phase of it, by your own confession, is so imperfect in itself that it requires to be constantly exchanged for some other, equally defective."

Not at all," answered Ellis, "each phase is good

in its time and place; but each becomes bad if it is pursued exclusively to the detriment of others."

"But is each good in itself? or, at least, is it more good than bad? You choose, in imagination, to dwell upon the good aspect of each; but in practice you would have to experience also the bad. Your hunting in trackless forests will involve exposure, fatigue, and hunger; your fighting in Madagascar, fever, wounds, and disillusionment; and so through all your chapter of accidents—for accidents they are at best, and never the substance of Good; rather, indeed, a substance of Evil, dogged by a shadow of Good."

"Oh!" cried Ellis, "what a horrid prosaic view—from an idealist, too! Why, the Bad is all part of the Good; one takes the rough with the smooth. Or rather the Good stands above what you call good and bad; it consists in the activity itself which feeds upon both alike. If I were Dennis I should say it is the synthesis of both."

"Well," said Leslie, "I never heard before of a synthesis produced by one side of the antithesis simply swallowing the other."

"Didn't you?" said Ellis. "Then you have a great deal yet to learn. This is known as the synthesis of the lion and the lamb."

"Oh, synthesis!" cried Parry. "Heaven save us from synthesis! What is it you are trying to say?"

"That's what I want to know," I said. "We seem to be coming perilously near to Dennis's position, that what we call Evil is mere appearance."

"Well," said Ellis, "extremes meet! Dennis arrived at his view by a denial of the world; I arrive at mine by an affirmation of it."

"But do you really think," I urged, "that everything in the world is good?"

"I think," he replied, "that everything may be made to minister to Good if you approach it in the proper way."

"That reads," said Audubon, "like an extract from a sermon."

"As I remarked before," replied Ellis, "extremes meet."

"But, Ellis," I protested, "do explain! How are you going to answer Leslie?"

"Leslie is really too young," he replied, "to be answerable at all. But if you insist on my being serious, what I meant to suggest is, that when our activity is freshest and keenest we find delight in what is called Evil no less than in what is called Good. The complexity of the world charms us, its 'downs' as well as its 'ups,' its abysses and glooms no less than its sunny levels. We would not alter it if we could; it is better than we could make it; and we accept it not merely with acquiescence but with triumph."

"Oh, do we!" said Audubon.

"We," answered Ellis, "not you! You, of course, do not accept anything."

"But who are 'we'?" asked Leslie.

"All of us," he replied, "who try to make an art of living. Yes, art, that is the word! To me life appears like a great tragi-comedy. It has its shadows as well as its lights, but we would not lose one of them, for fear of destroying the harmony of the whole. Call it good, or call it bad, no matter, so it is. The villain no less than the hero claims our applause; it would be dull without him. We can't afford to miss anything or anyone."

"In fact," cried Audubon, "'Konx Ompax! Totality!' You and Dennis are strangely agreed for once!"

"Yes," he replied, "but for very different reasons, as the judge said on the one occasion when he concurred with his colleagues. Dennis accepts the Whole because he finds it a perfect logical system; I, because I find it a perfect work of art. His prophet is Hegel; mine is Walt Whitman."

"Walt Whitman! And you profess to be an artist!"

"So was he, not in words but in life. One thing to him was no better nor worse than another; small and great, high and low, good and bad, he accepts them all, with the instinctive delight of an actual physical contact. Listen to him!" And he began to quote:

> "I do not call one greater and one smaller,
> "That which fills its period and place is equal to any.
> "I believe a leaf of grass is no less than the journey-work of the stars.
> "And the pismire is equally perfect, and a grain of sand, and the egg of the wren,
> "And the tree-toad is a 'chef-d'œuvre' for the highest;
> "And the running blackberry would adorn the parlours of heaven,
> "And the narrowest hinge in my hand puts to scorn all machinery,
> "And the cow-crunching with depressed head surpasses any statue,
> "And a mouse is miracle enough to stagger sextillions of infidels."

"That's all very well," objected Leslie, "though, of course, it's rather absurd; but it does not touch the question of evil at all."

"Wait a bit," cried Ellis, "he's ready for you there."

> "I am not the poet of goodness only, I do not decline to be the poet of wickedness also.
> "What blurt is this about virtue and about vice?
> "Evil propels me and reform of evil propels me, I stand indifferent,
> "My gait is no fault-finder's or rejector's gait,
> "I moisten the roots of all that grows."
>
> . . . .
>
> "This is the meal equally set, this is the meat for natural hunger,
> "It is for the wicked just the same as the righteous, I make appointment with all,
> "I will not have a single person slighted or kept away,
> "The kept-woman, spunger, thief are hereby invited,
> "The heavy-lipped slave is invited, the venerealee is invited;
> "There shall be no difference between them and the rest."

"That's rather strong," remarked Parry.

"Don't you like it?" Ellis inquired.

"I think I might like it if I were drunk."

"Ah, but a poet, you see, is always drunk!"

'Well, I unfortunately, am often sober; and then I find the sponger and the venerealee anything but agreeable objects."

"Besides," said Audubon, "though it's very good of Walt Whitman to invite us all, the mere fact of dining with him, however miscellaneous the company, doesn't alter the character of the dinner."

"No," cried Leslie, "and that's just the point Ellis has missed all through. Even if it be true that the world appears to him as a work of art, it doesn't appear so to the personages of the drama. What's play to him is grim earnest to them ; and, what's more, he himself is an actor not a mere spectator, and may have that fact brought home to him, any moment, in his flesh and blood."

"Of course!" replied Ellis, "and I wouldn't have it otherwise. The point of the position is that one should play one's part oneself, but play it as an artist with one's eye upon the total effect, never complaining of Evil merely because one happens to suffer, but taking the suffering itself as an element in the æsthetic perfection of the Whole."

"I should like to see you doing that," said Bartlett, rather brutally, "when you were down with a fit of yellow fever."

"Or shut up in a mad-house," said Leslie.

"Or working eight hours a day at business," said Audubon, "with the thermometer 100° in the shade."

"Oh well," answered Ellis, "those are the confounded accidents of our unhealthy habits of life."

"I am afraid," I said, "they are accidents very essential to the substance of the world."

"Besides," cried Parry, "there's the whole moral question, which you seem to ignore altogether. If there be any activity that is good, it must be, I suppose, the one that is right; and the activity you describe seems to have nothing to do with right and wrong."

"Right and wrong! Right and wrong!" echoed Ellis,

> "Das hör' ich sechzig Jahre wiederholen,
> Ich fluche drauf, aber verstohlen."

"You may curse as much as you like," replied Parry, "but you can hardly deny that there is an intimate connection between Good and Right."

Instead of replying Ellis began to whistle; so I took up Parry's point and said, "Yes, but what is the connection? My own idea is that Right is really a means to Good. And I should separate off all activity that is merely a means from that which is really an end in itself, and good."

"But is there any activity," objected Leslie, "which is not merely a means?"

"Oh yes," I said, "I should have thought so. Most men, it seems to me, are well enough content with what they are doing for its own sake; even though at the same time they have remoter ends in view, and if these were cut off would cease, perhaps, to take pleasure in the work of the moment. The attitude is not very logical, perhaps, but I think it is very common. Why else is it that men who believe and maintain that they only work in order to make money, nevertheless are so unwilling to retire when the money is made; or, if they do, are so often dissatisfied and unhappy?"

"Oh," said Audubon, "that is only because boredom is worse than pain. It is not that they find any satisfaction in their work; it's only that they find even greater distress in idleness."

"But, surely," I replied, "even you yourself would hardly maintain that there is nothing men do for its own sake, and because they take delight in it. If there were nothing else at least there is play—and I have known you play cricket yourself!"

"Known him play cricket!" cried Ellis. "Why,

if he had his way, he would do nothing else, except at the times when he was riding or shooting."

"Well," I said, "that's enough, for the moment, to refute him. And, in fact, I suppose none of us would seriously maintain that there is no form of activity which men feel to be good for its own sake, though the Good of course may be partial and precarious."

"No," said Ellis, "I should rather inquire whether there is any form which they pursue merely and exclusively as a means to something else."

"Oh, surely!" I said. "One might mention, for instance, the act of visiting the dentist. Or what is more important, and what, I suppose, Parry had in his mind, there is the whole class of activities which one distinguishes as moral."

"Do you mean to say," said Parry, "that moral action has no Good in itself but is only a means to some other Good?"

"I don't know," I replied; "I am rather inclined to think so. But it all depends upon how we define it."

"And how do you define it?"

"I should say that its specific quality consists in the refusal to seize some immediate and inferior Good with a view to the attainment of one that is remoter but higher."

"Oh, well, of course," cried Leslie, "if you define it so, your proposition follows of itself."

"So I thought," I said. "But how would you define it?"

"I should say it is a free and perfect activity in Good."

"In that case, it is of course the very activity we are in quest of, and we should come upon it, if we were successful, at the end of our inquiry. But I was supposing that the essence of morality is expressed in the word 'ought'; and in that I take to be implied the definition I suggested—namely, action pursued not for its own sake, but for the sake of something else."

"Oh, oh!" cried Dennis, "there I really must protest! I've kept silent as long as I possibly could; but when it comes to describing as a mere means the only kind of activity which is an end in itself——"

"The only kind that is an end in itself!" I repeated, in some dismay. "Is that really what you think?"

"Of course it is! why not?"

"I don't know. I have always supposed that, when we are doing what we ought, we are acting with a view to some ultimate Good."

"Well, I, on the contrary, believe that we ought absolutely, without reference to anything else. It is a unique form of activity, dependent on nothing but itself; and for anything we have yet shown, it may be the Good we are in quest of."

This suggestion, unexpected as it was, threw me into great perplexity. I did not see exactly how to meet it; yet it awakened no response in me, nor as I thought in any of the others. But while I was hesitating, Leslie began:

"Do you mean that the Good might consist simply in doing what we ought, without any other accompaniment or conditions?"

"Yes, I think it might."

"So that, for example, a man might be in possession of the Good, even while he was being racked or burnt alive, so long only as he was doing what he ought."

"Yes, I suppose he might be."

"It's a trifle paradoxical," said Ellis.

"In fact," added Bartlett, "it might be called nonsense."

"I don't see why," replied Dennis; "for we haven't yet shown that the Good is dependent on the things we call good."

"No," I said, "but we did show—or at least for the time being we agreed to admit—that it must have some relation to what we call goods; that they do somehow or other, and more or less, express its nature; and indeed our whole present inquiry is based upon the hypothesis that it is by examining goods that we may get to know something about the Good. So that I do not see how we can entertain an idea of Good which flatly contradicts all our experience of goods."

"Well," said Dennis, "I ought perhaps to modify the position. Let us say that the Good consists in the activity of doing what we ought, only that activity can't exist in its true perfection unless everybody participates in it at once. But if everybody participated in it, there would be no more burnings; and so Leslie's difficulty would not arise."

"Well," I said, "the modification is very radical! But even so, I don't know what to make of the position. For it is very difficult to conceive a society perpetually and exclusively occupied, so to speak, in 'oughting.' Just imagine the kind of life it would be—without pleasure, without business, without knowledge, without anything at all analogous to what we call good, purged wholly and completely of all that might taint the purity of the moral sense, of philanthropy, of friendship, of love, even, I suppose, of the love of virtue, a life simply of obligation, without anything to be obliged to except a law."

"But," he protested, "you are taking an absurd and impossible case."

"I am taking the case which you yourself put, when you said that Good consisted simply in doing what one ought, independently of all other accompaniment or condition. But perhaps that is not what you really meant?"

"No," he said; "of course, what I meant was that it is life according to the moral law that is Good; but I did not intend to separate the law from the life, and call it Good all by itself."

"But is the life the better for the law, in the sense, I mean, in which law involves constraint? Or would it not be better still if the same life were pursued freely for its own sake?"

"Perhaps so."

"But, then, in that case, the more we realized Good the less we should be aware of obligation. And would a life without conscious and felt obligation be a life specifically ethical, in the sense in which you seemed to be using the word?"

"I should think not; for 'ought' in the ethical sense does certainly seem to me to involve the idea of obligation."

"In that case it would seem to be truer to say

that activity is Good, not in so far as it is ethical but precisely in so far as it is not. At any rate, I should maintain that we come nearer to a realization of Good in the activities which we pursue without effort or friction, than in those which involve a struggle between duty and inclination."

"But the activities we pursue without effort or friction often enough are bad."

"No doubt; but some of them are good, and it is to those I should look for the best idea I could form of what Good might be."

"Well," he said, "go on! Once more I have entered my protest; and now I leave the road clear."

"The worst of you is," said Ellis, "that you always turn up in front! When we think we have passed you once for all, you take a short cut across the fields, and there you are in the middle of the road, with the same old story, that we're altogether on the wrong track."

"Well," said Dennis, sententiously, "I do my duty."

"And," replied Ellis, "no doubt you have your reward! Proceed!" he continued, turning to me.

"Well," I said, "I suppose I must try to go through to the end, though these tactics of Dennis make me very nervous. I shall suppose, however, that I have convinced him that it is not in ethical activity as such that we can expect to find the most perfect example of Good. And now I propose to examine in turn some other of our activities, starting with that which seems to be the most primitive of all."

"And which is that?"

"I was thinking of the activity of our bodily senses, our direct contact, so to speak, with objects, without the intermediation of reflection, through the touch, the sight, the hearing, and the rest. Is there anything in all this which we could call good?"

"Is there anything!" cried Ellis. "What a question to ask!" And he broke out with the lines from Browning's "Saul":

'Oh, the wild joys of living! the leaping from rock up to rock,
The strong rending of boughs from the fir-tree, the cool silver shock
Of the plunge in a pool's living water, the hunt of the bear,
And the sultriness showing the lion is couched in his lair.
And the meal, the rich dates yellowed over with gold dust divine,
And the locust-flesh steeped in the pitcher, the full draught of wine,
And the sleep in the dried river-channel where bulrushes tell
That the water was wont to go warbling so softly and well.
How good is man's life, the mere living! how fit to employ
All the heart and the soul and the senses for ever in joy."

The quotation seemed to loosen all tongues; and there followed a flood of such talk as may be heard in almost every company of Englishmen, in praise of sport and physical exercise, touched with a sentiment not far removed from poetry—the only poetry of which they are not half-ashamed. Audubon even joined in, forgetting for the moment his customary pose, and rhapsodizing with the rest over his favourite pursuits of snipe-shooting and cricket. Much of this talk was lost upon me, for I am nothing of a sportsman; but some touches there were that recalled experiences of my own, and for that reason, I suppose, have lingered in my memory. Thus, I recollect, some one spoke of skating on Derwentwater, the miles of black, virgin ice, the ringing and roaring of the skates, the sunset glow, and the moon rising full over the mountains; and another recalled a bathe on the shore of Ægina, the sun on the rocks and the hot scent of the firs, as though the whole naked body were plunged in some æthereal liqueur, drinking it in with every sense and at every pore, like a great sponge of sheer sensation. After some minutes of this talk, as I still sat silent, Ellis turned to me with the appeal, "But what about you, who are supposed to be our protagonist? Here are we all rhapsodizing and you sit silent. Have you nothing to contribute to your own theme?"

"Oh," I replied, "any experiences of mine would be so trivial they would be hardly worth recording. The most that could be said of them would be that they might, perhaps, illustrate more exactly than yours what one might call the pure Goods of sense. For, as far as I can understand, the delights you have been describing are really very complex. In addition to pleasures of mere sensation, there is clearly an æsthetic charm—you kept speaking of heather and sunrises, and colours and wide prospects; and then there is the satisfaction you evidently feel in skill, acquiring or acquired, and in the knowledge you possess of the habits of beasts and birds. All this, of course, goes beyond the delight of simple sense perception, though, no doubt, inextricably bound up with it. But what I was thinking of at first was something less complex and more elementary in which, nevertheless, I think we can detect Good—a Good of sheer unadulterated sensation. Think, for example, of the joys of a cold bath when one is dusty and hot! You will laugh at me, but sometimes when I have felt the water pouring down my back I have shouted to myself in my tub 'nunc dimittis.'"

They burst out laughing, and Ellis cried:

"You gross sensualist! And to think of all this being concealed behind that masque of austere philosophy!"

Then they set off again in praise of the delights of such simple sensations, and especially of those of the palate, instancing, I remember, the famous tale about Keats—how he covered his tongue and throat with cayenne pepper that he might enjoy, as he said, "the delicious coolness of claret in all its glory." And when this had gone on for some time, "Perhaps enough has been said," I began, "to illustrate this particular kind of Good. We have, I think, recognized to the full its merits; and we shall be equally ready, I suppose, to recognize its defects."

"I don't know about that," said Ellis. "I, for my part, at any rate, shall be very loth to dwell upon them. I sometimes think these are the only pure Goods."

"But at least," I replied, "you will admit that they are precarious. It is only at moments, and at moments that come and go without choice of ours, that this harmonious relation becomes established between our senses and the outer world. The very same things which at such times appear to be perfectly at one with ourselves, as if they had been made for us and we for them, we see and feel to have also a nature not only distinct but even alien and hostile to our own. The water which cools our skin and quenches our thirst also drowns; the fire which warms and comforts also burns; and so on through all the chapter—I need not weary you with details. Nature, you will agree, not only ministers to our bodies, she torments and destroys them; she is our foe in ways at least as varied and efficacious as she is our friend."

"But," objected Ellis, "that is only because we don't treat her properly; we have to learn how to manage her."

"Perhaps," I replied, "though I should prefer to say, we have to learn how to fight and subdue her. But in any case we have laid our finger here upon a defect in this first kind of Goods—they are, as I said, precarious. And the discovery of that fact, one might say, was the sword of the angel that drove man out of his imaginary Eden. For at first we may suppose him, (if Wilson will permit me to romance a little,) seizing every delight as it offered itself, under an instinctive impression that there were nothing but delights to be met with, eating when he was hungry, drinking when he was thirsty, sleeping when he was tired, and so on, in unquestioning trust of his natural impulses. But then, as he learnt by experience how evil follows good, and pleasure often enough is bought by pain, he would begin, would he not, instead of simply accepting Good where it is, to endeavour to create it where it is not, sacrificing often enough the present to the future, and rejecting many immediate delights for the sake of those more remote? And this involves a complete change in his attitude; for he is endeavouring now to establish by his own effort that harmony between himself and the world which he fondly hoped at first was immediately given."

"But," objected Wilson, "he never did hope anything of the kind. This reconstruction of the past is all imaginary."

"I dare say it may be," I replied, "but that is of little consequence, if it helps us to seize our point more clearly; for we are not at present writing history. Man, then, we will suppose, is thus set out upon what is, whether he knows it or not, his quest to create, since he is unable to find ready-made, a world of objects harmonious to himself. But in this quest has he been, should you say, successful?"

"More or less, I suppose," answered Parry, "for he is progressively satisfying his needs, even if they are never completely satisfied."

"Perhaps," I replied, "though I sometimes have my doubts. The relation of man to nature, I have thought, is very strange and obscure. It is as though he began with the idea that he had only to remove a few blemishes from her face to make her completely accordant with his desire. But no sooner has he gone to work than these surface blemishes, as he thought them, prove to have roots deeper than all his probings; the more he cuts away the more he exposes of an element radically alien to himself, terrible and incomprehensible, branching wide and striking deep, and throwing up from depths unknown those symptoms and symbols of itself which he mistook for mere superficial stains."

"Really," protested Parry, "I see no grounds for such a view."

"Perhaps not," I said, "but anyhow you will, I suppose, admit that a certain precariousness does attach to these Goods of sense, whether they be freely offered by nature or painfully acquired by the labour of man."

"Not necessarily," he objected, "for we are constantly reducing to order and routine what was once haphazard and uncontrolled. For the great mass of civilized men the primitive goods of life, food, shelter, clothing and the like, are practically secured against all chance."

"Are they?" cried Bartlett, "I admire your optimism!"

"And I too," I said. "But even granting that it were as you say, we are then met by this curious fact, that the Goods we really care about, in our practical activity, are never those that are secure but those that are precarious. As soon as we are safe against one risk we proceed to take another, so that there is always a margin, as it were, of precarious Goods, and those exactly the ones which we hold most precious."

"In fact," said Audubon, "as soon as you get your Good it ceases to be good. That's precisely what I am always saying."

"Then," I said, "there is the less need to labour the point. One way or other, it seems, either because they are difficult to secure, or because, when secured, they lose their specific quality. Goods of this kind are caught in the wheels of chance and change, whether they be offered to man by the free gift of Nature, or wrung from her in the sweat of his brow. In other words, they are, as I said, precarious. And now, have they any other defects?"

"Have they any?" cried Leslie, "why they have nothing else!"

"Well," I said, "but what in particular?"

"Oh," he replied, "it's all summed up, I suppose, in the fact that they are Goods of sense, and not of intellect or of imagination."

"Is it then," I asked, "a defect in content that you are driving at? Do you mean that they satisfy only a part of our nature, not the whole? For that, I suppose, would be equally true of the other Goods you mentioned, such as those of the intellect."

"Yes," he replied, "but it is the inferior part to which the Goods we are speaking of appeal."

"Perhaps; but in what respect inferior?"

"Why, simply as the body is inferior to the soul."

"But how is that? You will think me very stupid, but the more I think of it the less I understand this famous distinction between body and soul, and the relation of one to the other."

"I doubt," said Wilson, "whether there is a distinction at all."

"I don't say that," I replied. "I only say that I can't understand it; and I should be thankful, if possible, to keep it out of our discussion."

"So should I!" said Wilson.

"Well, but," Leslie protested, "how can we?"

"I think perhaps we might," I said. "For instance, in the case before us, why should we not try directly to define that specific property of the Goods of sense which, according to you, constitutes their defect, without having recourse to these difficult terms body and soul at all?"

"Well," he agreed, "we might try."

"What, then," I said, "do you suggest?"

He hesitated a little, and then began in a tentative kind of way:

"I think what I feel about these Goods is that we are somehow their slaves; they possess us, instead of our possessing them. They come upon us we hardly know how or whence; they satisfy our desires we can't tell why; our relation to them seems to be passive rather than active."

"And that, you think, would not be the case with a true and perfect Good?"

"No, I think not."

"How, then, should we feel towards such a Good?"

"We should feel, I think, that it was somehow an expression of ourselves, and we of it; that it was its nature and its whole nature to present itself as a Good and our nature and our whole nature to experience it as such. There would be nothing in it alien to us and nothing in us alien to it."

"Whereas in the case of Goods of sense——?"

"Whereas in their case," he said, "surely nothing of the kind applies. For these Goods appear to arise in things and under circumstances which have quite another nature than that of being good for us. It is not the essence of water to quench our thirst, of fire to cook for us, or of the sun to give us light——"

"Or of cork-trees to stop our ginger-beer bottles," added Ellis.

"Quite so," he continued; "in every case these things that do us good are also quite as ready to do us harm, and, for that matter, to do innumerable things which have no relation to us at all. So that the goodness they have in them, so far as it is goodness to our senses, they have, as it were, only by accident; and we feel that essentially either they are not Goods, or their goodness is something beyond and different from that which is revealed to sense."

"Your quarrel, then," I said, "with the Goods of sense, so far as I understand you, is that they inhere, as it were, in a substance which, so far as we can tell, is indifferent to Good, or at any rate to Good of that kind?"

"Yes."

"Whereas a true Good, you think, must be good in essence and substance?"

"Yes; don't you think so too?"

"I do," I replied, "but how about the others?"

Dennis assented, and the others did not object, not appearing, indeed, to have attended much to the argument. So I continued, "We have then, so far, discovered in this class of Goods, two main defects, the first, that they are precarious; the second, which is closely connected with the other, and is in fact, I suppose, its explanation, that they are, shall we say, accidental, understanding the word in the sense we have just defined. Now, let us see if we cannot find any class of Goods similar to these, but free from their defects."

"But similar in what respect," he asked, "if they are not to have similar defects?"

"Similar, I meant, in being direct presentations to sense."

"But are there any such Goods?"

"I think so," I said. "What do you say to works of Art? These, are they not, are direct presentations to sense? Yet such that it is their whole nature and essence on the one hand to be beautiful, and to that extent Good—for I suppose you will admit that the Beautiful is a kind of Good; and on the other hand, if I may dare to say so, to be, in a certain sense, eternal."

"Eternal!" cried Ellis. "I only wish they were! What wouldn't we give for the works of Polygnotus and Apelles!"

"Oh yes," I said, "of course, in that way, regarded as material objects, they are as perishable as all the works of nature. But I was talking of them as Art, not as mere things; and from that point of view, surely, each is a moment, or a series of moments, cut away, as it were, from the contact of chance or change and set apart in a timeless world of its own, never of its own nature, to pass into something else, but only through the alien nature of the matter to which it is bound."

"What do you mean?" cried Parry. "I am quite at sea."

"Perhaps," I said, "you will understand the point better if I give it you in the words of a poet."

And I quoted the well-known stanzas from Keats' "Ode on a Grecian Urn":

"Heard melodies are sweet, but those unheard
  Are sweeter; therefore, ye soft pipes, play on;
Not to the sensual ear, but, more endear'd,
  Pipe to the spirit ditties of no tone:

Fair youth beneath the trees, thou canst not leave
  Thy song, nor ever can those trees be bare;
    Bold lover, never, never canst thou kiss,
Though winning near the goal—yet, do not grieve;
    She cannot fade, though thou hast not thy bliss,
  For ever wilt thou love and she be fair!

"Ah, happy, happy boughs! that cannot shed
  Your leaves, nor ever bid the spring adieu;
And, happy melodist, unwearied,
  For ever piping songs for ever new;
More happy love! more happy, happy love!
  For ever warm and still to be enjoyed,
    For ever panting and for ever young;
All breathing human passion far above,
  That leaves a heart high-sorrowful and cloy'd,
    A burning forehead, and a parching tongue."

"Well," said Parry, when I had done, "that's very pretty; but I don't see how it bears on the argument."

"I think," I replied, "that it illustrates the point I wanted to make. Part, I mean, of the peculiar charm of works of Art consists in the fact that they arrest a fleeting moment of delight, lift it from our sphere of corruption and change, and fix it like a star in the eighth heaven."

"Yes," said Ellis, "we grant you that."

"Or at least," added Parry, "we don't care to dispute it."

"And the other point which I want to make is, I think, clearer still—that the Good of works of Art, that is to say their Beauty, results from the very principle of their nature, and is not a mere accident of circumstances."

"Of course," said Leslie, "their Beauty is their only *raison d'être.*"

"And yet," I went on, "they are still Goods of sense, and so far resemble the other Goods of which we were speaking before."

"Yes," said Dennis, "but with what a difference! That is the point I have been waiting to come to."

"What point?" I asked.

"Why," he said, "in the case of what you call Goods of sense, in their simplest and purest form, making abstraction from all æsthetic and other elements—as in the example you gave of a cold bath—the relation of the object to the sense is so simple and direct, that really, if we were to speak accurately, we should have, I think, to say, that so far as the perception of Good is concerned the object is merged in the subject, and what you get is simply a good sensation."

"Perhaps," I agreed, "that is how we ought to put it. But at the time I did not think it necessary to be so precise."

"But it has become necessary now, I think," he replied, "if we are to bring out a characteristic of works of Art which will throw light, I believe, on the general nature of Good."

"What characteristic is that?"

"Why," he replied, "when we come to works of Art, the important thing is the object, not the subject; if there is any merging of the one in the other, it is the subject that is merged in the object, not *vice versa*. We have to contemplate the object, anyhow, as having a character of its own; and it is to this character that I want to draw attention."

"In what respect?"

'In respect that every work of Art, and, for that matter, every work of nature—so far as it can be viewed æsthetically—comprises a number of elements necessarily connected in a whole; and this necessary connection is the point on which we ought to insist."

"But necessary how?" asked Wilson. "Do you mean logically necessary?"

"No," he replied, "æsthetically. I mean, that we have a direct perception that nothing in the work could be omitted or altered without destroying the whole. This, at any rate, is the ideal; and it holds, more or less, in proportion as the work is more or less perfect. Everyone, I suppose, who understands these things would agree to that."

No one seemed inclined to dispute the statement; certainly I was not, myself; so I answered, "No doubt what you say is true of works of Art; but will your contention be that it is also true of Good in general?"

"Yes," he said, "I think so, in so far at least as Good is to be conceived as comprising a number of elements. For no one, I suppose, would imagine that such elements might be thrown together haphazard and yet constitute a good whole."

"I suppose not," I agreed, "and, if you are right, what we seem to have arrived at is this: among the works which man creates in his quest of the Good, there is one class, that of works of Art, which, in the first place, may be said, in a sense, to be not precarious, seeing that by their form, through which they are Art, they are set above the flux of time, though by their matter, we admit, they are bound to it. And, in the second place, the Good which they have, they have by virtue of their essence; Good is their substance, not an accident of their changing relations. And, lastly, being complex wholes, the parts of which they are composed are bound together in necessary connection. These characteristics, at any rate, we have discovered in works of Art: and no doubt many more might be discoverable. But now, let us turn to the other side, and consider the defects in which this class of Goods is involved."

"Ah!" cried Bartlett, "when you come to that, I have something to say."

"Well," I said, "what is it? We shall be glad of any help."

"It can be summed up," he replied, "in a single word. Whatever may be the merits of a work of Art—and they may be all that you say—it has this one grand defect—it isn't real!"

"Real!" cried Leslie. "What is real? The word's the plague of my life! People use it as if they meant something by it, something very tremendous and august, and when you press them they never know what it is. They talk of 'real life'—real life! what is it? As if one life wasn't as real as another!"

"Oh, as to real life," said Ellis, "I can tell you what that is. Real life is the shady side of life."

"Nonsense," said Parry, "real life is the life of men of the world."

"Or," retorted Ellis, "more generally, it is the life of the person speaking, as opposed to that of the person to whom he speaks."

"Well, but," I interposed, "it is not 'real life' that is our present concern, but Bartlett's meaning when he used the word 'real.' In what sense is Art not real?"

"Why," he replied, "by your own confession Art is something ideal. It is beautiful, it is good, it is lifted above chance and change; its connection with matter, that is to say with reality, is a kind of flaw, an indecency from which we discreetly turn our eyes. The real world is nothing of all this; on the contrary, it is ugly, brutal, material, coarse, and bad as bad can be!"

"I don't see that it is at all!" cried Leslie, "and, even if it were, you have no right to assume that that is the reality of it. How do you know that its reality doesn't consist precisely in the Ideal, as all poets and philosophers have thought? And, in that case, Art would be more real than what you would call Reality, because it would represent the essence of the world, the thing it would like to be if it could, and is, so far as it can. That was Aristotle's view, anyhow."

"Then all I can say is," replied Bartlett, "that I don't agree with Aristotle! Anyhow, even if Art represents what the world would like to be, it certainly doesn't represent what it is."

"I don't know; surely it does, sometimes," said Parry, "for instance, there's the realistic novel!"

"Oh, that!" cried Ellis. "That's the most ideal of all—only it's apt to be such bad idealism!"

"Anyhow," said Bartlett, "in so far as it is real, it's not Art, in the sense in which we have been using the word."

I began to be afraid that we should drift away into a discussion of realism in Art. So, to recall the conversation to the point at issue, I turned to Bartlett, and said:

"Your criticism seems to me to be fair enough as far as it goes. You say that the world of Art is a world by itself; that side by side of it, and unaffected by it, moves the world of what you call real life. And that whatever be the relation between the two worlds, whether we are to say that the one imitates the other, or interprets it, or idealizes it, it does not, in any case, set it aside. Art is a refuge from life, not a substitute for it; a little blessed island in the howling sea of fact. Its Good is thus only a partial Good; whereas the true Good, I suppose, would be somehow universal."

"Still," said Leslie, "as far as it goes it is a Good without blemish."

"I am not so sure," I said, "even of that. I am inclined to think that Bartlett's criticism, if we squeeze it tight, will yield us more than we have yet got out of it—perhaps even more than he knows is in it."

"You don't mean to say," cried Bartlett, "that you are coming over to my side!"

"Yes," I said, "like a spy to the enemy's camp to see where your strength really lies."

"I have no objection," he replied, "if it ends in your discovering new defences for me."

"Well," I said, "we shall see. Anyhow, this is what I had in my mind. We were saying just now that when people talk about 'real life,' the 'real world,' and so on, they are not always very clear as to what they mean. But one thing, I think, perhaps they have obscurely in their heads—that the Real is something from which you cannot escape; something which forces itself upon you without reference to choice or desire, having a nature of its own which may or may not conform, more or less to yours, but in any case is distinct and independent. That is why they would say, for example, that the illusions of a madman are not real, meaning that they do not represent real things, however vivid their appearance may be, because they are the productions merely of his own consciousness; whereas the very same appearances presented to a sane man would be called without hesitation real, because they would be conceived to proceed from objects having an independent nature of their own. Something of this kind, I suppose, is included in the notion 'real' as it is held by ordinary people."

"Perhaps," said Leslie, "but what then? And how does it bear upon Art?"

"I am not sure," I replied, "but it occurred to me that works of Art, though of course they are real objects, are such that a certain violence, as it were, has been done to their reality in our interest. What I mean will be best understood, I think, if we put ourselves for the moment into the position of the artist. To him certain materials are presented which of course are real in our present acceptation of the term, being such as they are of their own nature, without any dependence upon him. Upon these materials he flings himself, and shapes them according to his desire, impressing, as it were, his own nature upon theirs, till they confront him as a kind of image of himself in an alien stuff. So far, then, he has a Good, and a Good presented to him as real; but for the Goodness of this reality he is himself responsible. In so far as it is, so to speak, merely real, it has still the nature which was first presented to him, before he began his work—a nature indifferent, if not opposed, to all his operations, as is shown by the fact that it changes and passes away into something else, just as it would have done if he had never touched it. To this nature he has, as I said, done a certain violence in order to stamp upon it the appearance of Good; but the Good is still, in a sense, only an appearance; the reality of the thing remains independent and alien. So that what the man has found, in so far as he has found Good, is after all only a form of himself; and one can conceive him feeling a kind of despair, like that of Wotan in the Walküre, when in his quest for a free, substantial, self-subsistent Good he finds after all, for ever, nothing but images of himself:

> 'Das Andre, das ich ersehne,
> Das Andre, erseh' ich nie.'

I don't know whether what I am saying is intelligible, for I find it rather hard to put it into words."

"Yes," he said, "I think I understand. But what you are saying, so far as it is true, seems to be true only for the artist himself. To all others the work of Art must appear as something independent of themselves."

"True," I said, "and yet I think that they too feel, or might be made to feel if it were brought home to them, this same antagonism between the nature of the stuff and the form that has been given to it. The form will seem from this point of view something factitious and artificial given to the stuff, not indeed by themselves, but by one like themselves, and in their interest. They will contrast, perhaps, as is often done, a picture of the landscape with the landscape itself. The picture, they will say, however beautiful, is not a 'natural' Good, not a real Good, not a Good in its own right; it is a kind of makeshift produced by human effort, beautiful, if you will, admirable, if you will, to be sought, to be cherished, to be loved in default of a better, with the best faculties of brain and soul, but still not that ultimate thing we wanted, that Good in and of itself, as well as through and for us, Good by its own nature apart from our interposition, self-moved, self-determined, self-dependent, and in which alone our desires could finally rest.—Don't you think that some such feeling may, perhaps, be at the bottom of Bartlett's criticism of Art as unreal?"

Bartlett laughed. "If so," he said, "it is quite unknown to myself. For to tell the truth, I have not understood a word that you have said."

"Well," I said, "in that case, at any rate you can't disagree with me. But what do the others think?" And I turned to Dennis and Leslie, for Wilson and Parry did not seem to be attending. Leslie assented with enthusiasm. But Dennis shook his head.

"I don't know," he said, "what to think about all that. It seems to me rather irrelevant to the work of Art as such."

"Perhaps," I said, "but surely not to the work of Art as Good? Or do you not agree with me that the true Good must be such purely of its own nature?"

"Perhaps so," he replied; "it wants thinking over. But in any case I agree with you so far, that I should never place the Good in Art."

"In what then?"

"I should be much more inclined to place it in Knowledge."

"In Knowledge!" I repeated. "That seems to me very strange!"

"But why strange?" he said. "Surely there is good authority for the view. It was Aristotle's for example, and Spinoza's."

"I know," I replied, "and I used to think it was also mine. But of late I have come to realize more clearly what Knowledge is; and now I see, or seem to see, that whatever its value may be, it is something that falls very far short of Good."

"Why," he said, "what is your idea of Knowledge?"

"You had better ask Wilson," I replied, "it is he who has instructed me."

"Very well," he said, "I appeal to Wilson."

And Wilson, nothing loth, enunciated his definition of Knowledge.

"Knowledge," he said, "is the description and summing up in brief formulæ of the routine of our perceptions."

"There!" I exclaimed. "No one, I suppose, would identify that with Good?"

"But"—objected Dennis—"in the first place, I don't understand the definition; and, in the second place, I don't agree with it."

"As to understanding it," replied Wilson, "there need be no difficulty there. You have only to seize clearly one or two main positions. First, that Knowledge is of perceptions only, not of things in themselves; secondly, that these perceptions occur in fixed routines; thirdly . . ."

"But," interrupted Dennis, "what is a perception? I suppose it's a perception of something?"

"No," he said, "I don't know that it is."

"What then? Simply a state in me?"

"Very likely."

"Then does nothing exist except my states?"

"Nothing else exists primarily for you."

"Then what about the world before I existed, and after I cease to exist?"

"You infer such a world from your states."

"Then there is something besides my states—this world which I infer; and that, I suppose, and not merely my perceptions, is the reality of which I have knowledge?"

"Not exactly," he replied, "the fact is . . ."

"I don't think," I interrupted, "that we ought to plunge into a discussion of the nature of Reality. It is Good with which we are at present concerned."

"But," said Dennis, "we wanted to find out the connection of Knowledge with Good; and to do so we must first discover what Knowledge is."

"Well then," I said, "let us first take Wilson's account of Knowledge, and see what he makes of that with regard to Good; and then we will take yours, and see what we make of that. And if we don't find that either satisfies the requirements of Good we will leave Knowledge and go on to something else.'

"Very well," he replied "I am content, so long as I get my chance."

"You shall have your chance. But first we will take Wilson. And I dare say he will not keep us long. For you will hardly maintain, I suppose," I continued, turning to him, "that Knowledge, as you define it, could be identified with Good?"

"I don't know," he said; "to tell the truth, I don't much believe in Good, in any absolute sense. But that Knowledge, as I define it, is a good thing, I have no doubt whatever."

"Neither have I," I replied; "but good, as it seems to me, mainly as a means, in so far as it enables us to master Nature."

"Well," he said, "and what greater Good could there be?"

"I don't dispute the greatness of such a Good. I merely wish to point out that if we look at it so, it is in the mastery of Nature that the Good in question consists, and not in the Knowledge itself. Or should you say that there is Good in the scientific activity itself, quite apart from any practical results to which it may lead?"

"Certainly," he replied, "and the former, in my opinion, is the higher and more ideal Good."

"This activity itself of inventing brief formulæ to resume the routine of our perceptions?"

"Yes."

"Well, but what *is* the Good of it? That is what it is so hard for a layman to get hold of. Does it consist in the discovery of Reality? For that, I could understand, would be good."

"No," he said, "for we do not profess to touch Reality. We deal merely with our perceptions."

"So that when, for example, you conceive such

and such a perfect fluid, or whatever you call it, and such and such motions in it, you do not suppose this fluid to be real."

"No. It is merely a conception by means of which we are enabled to give an account of the order in which certain of our perceptions occur. But it is very satisfactory to be able to give such an account."

"I suppose it must be," I said, "but once more, could you say more precisely wherein the satisfaction consists? Is it, perhaps, in the discovery of necessary connections?"

"No," he said, "we don't admit necessity. We admit only an order which is, as a matter of fact, regular."

"You say, for example, that it so happens that all bodies do move in relation to one another in the way summed up in the law of gravitation; but that you see no reason why they should?"

"Yes."

"But . . ." began Dennis, who had found difficulty all this time in restraining himself.

"One moment!" I pleaded, "let Wilson have his say." And turning to him I continued: "If, then, the satisfaction to be derived from scientific activity does not consist in the discovery of Reality, nor yet in that of necessary connection, wherein should you say, does it consist? Perhaps in the regulating of expectation?"

"What do you mean by that?"

"I mean, that it is painful for us to live in a world in which we don't know what to expect; it excites not only our fears and apprehensions, but also a kind of intellectual disgust. And, conversely, it is a relief and a pleasure to discover an order among our experiences, not only because it enables us the better to utilize them for our ends (for that belongs to the practical results of science), but because in itself we prefer order to disorder, even if no other advantage were to be got out of it."

"I don't know that we do!" objected Ellis, "it depends on the kind of order. An order of dull routine is far more intolerable than a disorder of splendid possibilities! Ask the Oriental why he objects to British rule! Simply because it is regular! He prefers the chances of rapine, violent and picturesque, to the dreary machine-like depredations of the tax-collector."

"Yes," I said, "but there you take in a number of complex factors. I was thinking merely of the Good to be got out of scientific activity as such. And I think there is an intellectual satisfaction in the discovery of order, even though it be dissociated from necessity."

"No doubt there is," said Wilson, "but I shouldn't say that is the only reason for our delight in Knowledge. The fact is, Knowledge is an extension of experience, and is good simply as such. The sense of More and still More beyond what has yet been discovered, of new facts, new successions, new combinations, of ever fresh appeals to our interest, our wonder, our admiration, the mere excitement of discovery for its own sake, quite apart from anything else to which it may lead, a dash of adventure, too, a heightening of life—that is what is the real spur to science and, to my mind, its sufficient justification."

"But," I objected, "that is rather an account of the general process of Experience than of the special one of Knowledge. No doubt there is an attraction in all activity—Ellis has already expounded it; and all experience involves a kind of Knowledge; but what we wanted to get at was the special attraction of scientific activity; and that seems to be, so far as I can see, simply the discovery of order."

"Well," he said, "if you like—what then?"

"Why, then," I said, "we can easily see the defect in this kind of activity, when viewed from the standpoint of Good."

"What is it?"

"Why, clearly, that that in which we discover the order may be bad. There is a science of disease as well as of health; and an activity concerned with the Bad could hardly be purely good, even though it were a discovery of order in the Bad. Or do you think that if all men were diseased, they would nevertheless be in possession of the Good, if only they had perfect knowledge of the laws of disease?"

"No," he said, "of course not. We have to take into account, not only the character of Knowledge, but the character of the object known."

"Quite so, that is my point. You agree then with me that Knowledge may be in various ways good, but that in so far as it is, or may be knowledge of Bad, it cannot be said by itself to constitute the Good."

"I think," he agreed, "that I might admit that."

"Well, then," I said, "let us leave it there. And now, what has Dennis to say?"

"Ah!" he said, "you unmuzzle me at last. It

has really been very hard to sit by in silence and listen to these heresies without a protest."

"Heresies!" retorted Wilson, "if it comes to that, which of us is the heretic?"

"What," I asked, "is the point of disagreement?"

"It's a fundamental one. On Wilson's view, Knowledge is merely the discovery of order among our perceptions. If that were all, I shouldn't value it much. But on my view, it is the discovery of necessary connection; and in the necessity lies the fascination."

"But where," argued Wilson, "do you find your necessity? All that is really given is succession. The necessity is merely what we read into the facts."

"Not at all! The necessity is 'given,' as you call it, as much as anything else, if only you choose to look for it. The type of all Knowledge is mathematical knowledge; and all mathematical knowledge is necessary."

"But it is all based on assumptions."

"That may be; but granting the assumptions, it deduces from them necessary consequences. And all true science is of that type. A law of Nature is not a mere description of a routine; it's a statement that, given such and such conditions, such and such results follow of necessity."

"Still, you admit that the conditions have to be given! Everything is based ultimately on certain successions and coincidences of which all that can be said is simply that they exist, without any possibility of getting behind them."

"I don't know about that," he said, "but at any rate it would be the ideal of Knowledge to establish necessary connections throughout; so that, given any one phenomenon of the universe, all the rest would inevitably follow. And it is only in so far as it progresses towards this consummation that Knowledge is Knowledge at all. A routine simply given without internal coherence is to my mind a contradiction in terms; either the routine is necessary, or it's not a routine at all, but at best a mere appearance of a routine."

"I think," I interposed, "we must leave you and Wilson to fight this out in private. At present, let us assume that your conception of Knowledge is the true one, as we did with his, and examine it from the point of view of the Good. Your conception, then, to begin with, seems to me to be involved in the same defect we have already noted—namely, that it may be knowledge of Bad just as much as knowledge of Good. And I suppose you would hardly maintain, any more than Wilson did, that the Good may consist in knowledge of Bad?"

"But," he objected, "I protest altogether against this notion that there is Knowledge on the one hand and something of which there is knowledge on the other. True Knowledge, if ever we could attain to it, would be a unique kind of activity, in which there would be no distinction, or at least no antagonism, between thinking on the one hand and the thing thought on the other."

"I don't know," I said, "that I quite understand. Have we in fact any knowledge of that kind, that might serve as a kind of type of what you mean?"

"Yes," he replied, "I think we have. For example, if we are dealing with pure number, as in arithmetic, we have an object which is somehow native to our thought, commensurate with it, or however you like to put it; and it is the same with other abstract notions, such as substance and causation."

"I see," I said. "And on the other hand, the element which is alien to thought, and which is the cause of the impurity of most of what we call knowledge, is the element of sense—the something given, which thought cannot, as it were, digest, though it may dress and serve it up in its own sauce?"

"Yes," he said, "that is my idea."

"So that knowledge, to be perfect, must not be of sense, but only of pure thought, as Plato suggested long ago?"

"Yes."

"And such a knowledge, if we could attain it, you would call the Good?"

"I think so."

"Well," I said, "in the first place, I have to point out that such a Good (if it be one) implies an existence not merely better than that of which we have an experience, but radically and fundamentally different. For our whole life is bathed in sense. Not only are we sunk in it up to the neck, but the greater part of the time our heads are under too,—in fact most of us never get them out at all; it is only a few philosophers every now and again who emerge for a moment or two into sun and air, to breathe that element of pure thought which is too fine even for them, except as a rare indulgence. At other times, they too must be content with the grosser atmosphere which is the common sustenance of common men."

"Well," he said, "but what of that? We have not been maintaining that the Good is within easy reach of all."

"No," cried Ellis. "But even if it were, and were such as you describe it, very few people would care to put out their hands to take it. I, at any rate, for my part can see hardly a vestige of Good in the kind of activity I understand you to mean. It is as though you should say, that Good consists in the perpetual perception that $2 + 2 = 4$."

"But that is an absurd parody. For the point of knowledge would be, that it would be a closed circle of necessary connections. One would move in it, as in infinity, with a motion that is also rest, central at once and peripheral, free and yet bound by law. That is my ideal of a perfect activity!"

"In form, perhaps," I said, "but surely not in content! For what, in fact, in our experience comes nearest to what you describe? I suppose the movement of a logic like Hegel's?"

"Yes; only that, of course, is imperfect, full of lapses and flaws!"

"But even if it were perfect," cried Ellis, "would it be any the better? Imagine being deprived of the whole content of life—of nature, of history, of art, of religion, of everything in which we are really interested; imagine being left to turn for ever, like a squirrel in a cage, or rather like the idea of a squirrel in the idea of a cage, round and round the wheel of these hollow notions, without hands, without feet, without anything anywhere by which we could lay hold of a something that is not thought, a something solid, resistant, palpitating, 'luscious and aplomb,' as Walt Whitman might say, a sense, a flesh, call it what you will, the unintelligible, but still the indispensable, that which, even if it be bad, we cannot afford to miss, and which, if it be not the Good itself, the Good must somehow include!"

Dennis appeared to be somewhat struck by this way of putting the matter. "But," he urged, "my difficulty is that if you admit sense, or anything analogous to it, anything at once directly presented and also alien to thought, you get, as you said yourself, something which is unintelligible; and a Good which is not intelligible will be, so far, not good."

"But," I said, "what do you mean by intelligible?"

"I think," he replied, "that I mean two things, both of which must be present. First, that there shall be a necessary connection among the elements presented; and secondly, that the elements themselves should be of such a kind as to be, as it were, transparent to that which apprehends them, so that it asks no questions as to what they are or whence they come, but accepts them naturally and as a matter of course, with the same inevitability as it accepts its own being."

"And these conditions, you think, are fulfilled by the objects of thought as you defined them?"

"I think so."

"I am not so sure of that," I said, "it would require a long discussion. But, anyhow, you also seemed to admit, when Ellis pressed you, that thought of that kind could hardly be identified absolutely with Good."

"I admit," he replied, "that there are difficulties in that view."

"But at the same time the Good, whatever it be, ought to be intelligible in the sense you have explained?"

"I should say so."

"And so should I. But now, the question is, can we not conceive of any other kind of object, which might have, on the one hand, the intelligibility you ascribe to pure ideas, and on the other, that immediate something, 'luscious and aplomb,' to borrow Ellis's quotation, which he desiderated as a constituent of the Good?"

"I don't know," he said, "perhaps we might. What is it you have in your mind?"

"Well," I replied, "let us recur for a moment to works of art. In them we have, to begin with, directly presented elements other than mere ideas."

"No doubt."

"And further, these elements, we agreed, have a necessary connection one with the other."

"Yes, but not logically necessary."

"No doubt, but still a necessary connection. And it is the necessity of the connection, surely, that is important; the character of the necessity is a secondary consideration."

"Perhaps."

"One condition, then, of intelligibility is satisfied by a work of art. But how is it with the other? How is it with the elements themselves? Are they transparent, to use your phrase, to that which apprehends them?"

"Certainly not, for they are mere sense—of all things the most obscure and baffling."

"And yet," I replied, "not mere sense, for they are sense made beautiful; as beautiful, they are akin to us, and, so far, intelligible."

"You suggest, then, that Beauty is akin to something in us, in a way analogous to that in which, according to me, ideas are akin to thought?"

"It seems so to me. In so far as a thing is beautiful it does not, I think, demand explanation, but only in so far as it is something else as well."

"Perhaps. But anyhow, inasmuch as a work of art is also sense, so far at least it is not intelligible."

"True; and here we come by a new path upon the defect which we noticed before in works of art—that their Beauty, or Goodness, is not essential to their whole nature, but is something imposed, as it were, on an alien stuff. And it is this alien element that we now pronounce to be unintelligible."

"Yes; and so, as we agreed before, we cannot pronounce works of art to be absolutely good."

"No. But what are we to do then? Where are we to turn? Is there nothing in our experience to suggest the kind of object we seem to want?"

No one answered. I looked round in vain for any help, and then, in a kind of despair, moved by I know not what impulse, I made a direct appeal to Audubon.

"Come!" I cried, "you have said nothing for the last hour! I am sure you must have something to suggest."

"No," he said, "I haven't. Your whole way of dealing with these things is a mystery to me. I can't conceive, for example, why you have never once referred all through to what I should have thought was the best Good we know—if, indeed, we know any Good at all."

"What do you mean?"

"Why," he said, "one's relations to persons. They're the only things that I think really worth having—if anything were worth having."

A light suddenly broke on me, and I cried, "Yes! an idea!"

"Well," said Ellis, "what is it, you man of forlorn hopes?"

"Why," I said, "suppose the very object we are in search of should be found just there?"

"Where?"

"Why, in persons!"

"Persons!" he repeated. "But what persons? Any, every, all?"

"Wait one moment," I cried, "and don't confuse me! Let me approach the matter properly."

"Very well," he said, "you shan't be hurried! You shall have your chance."

"Let us remind ourselves, then," I proceeded, "of the point we had reached. The Good, we agreed, so far as we have been able to form a conception of it, must be something immediately presented, and presented in such a way, that it should be directly intelligible—intelligible not only in the relations that obtain between its elements, but also in the substance, so to speak, of the elements themselves. Of such intelligibility we had a type, as Dennis maintained, in the objects of pure thought, ideas and their relations. But the Good, we held, could not consist in these. It must be something, we felt, somehow analogous to sense, and yet it could not be sense, for sense did not seem to be intelligible. But now, when Audubon spoke, it occurred to me that perhaps we might find in persons what we want. And that is what I should like to examine now."

"Well," said Ellis, "proceed."

"To begin with, then, a person, I suppose we shall agree, is not sense, though he is manifested through sense."

"What does that mean?" said Wilson.

"It means only, that a person is not his body, although we know him through his body."

"If he isn't his body," said Wilson, "he is probably only a function of it."

"Oh!" I said, "I know nothing about that. I only know that when we talk of a person, we don't mean merely his body."

"No," said Ellis, "but we certainly mean also his body. Heaven save me from a mere naked soul, 'ganz ohne Körper, ganz abstrakt,' as Heine says."

"But, at any rate," I said, "let me ask you, for the moment, to consider the soul apart from the body."

"The soul," cried Wilson, "I thought we weren't to talk about body and soul."

"Well," I said, "I didn't intend to, but I seem to have been driven into it unawares."

"But what do you mean by the soul?"

"I mean," I replied, "what I suppose to be the proper object of psychology—for even people who object to the word 'soul' don't mind talking (in Greek, of course) of the science of the soul. Anyhow, what I mean is that which thinks and feels and wills."

"Well, but what about it?" said Ellis.

"The first thing about it is that it is, as it seems to me, of all things the most intelligible."

"I should have said," Wilson objected, "that it was of all things the least."

"Yes; but we are probably thinking of different things. What you have in your mind is the connection of this thing which you refuse to call the soul, with the body, the genesis and relations of its various faculties, the measurement of its response to stimuli, and all the other points which are examined in books of psychology. All that I agree is very unintelligible; I, at least, make no profession of understanding it. But what I meant was, that looking at persons as we know them in ordinary life, or as they are shown to us in literature and art, they really are intelligible to us in the same way that we are intelligible to ourselves."

"And how is that?"

"Why, through motives and passions. There is, I suppose, no feeling or action of which human beings are capable, from the very highest to the very lowest, which other human beings may not sympathetically understand, through the mere fact that they have the same nature. They will understand more or less according as they have more or less sympathy and insight; but in any case they are capable of understanding, and it is the business of literature and art to make them understand."

"That is surely a curious use of the word 'understand.'"

"But it is the one, I think, which is important for us. At any rate, what I mean is that the object presented is so akin, not indeed (as in the case of ideas) merely to our thought, but to our whole complex nature, that it does not demand explanation."

"What!" cried Audubon. "Well, all I can say is that most of the people I, at any rate, come across do most emphatically demand explanation. I don't see why they're there, or what they're doing, or what they're for. Their existence is a perpetual problem to me! And what's worse, probably my existence is the same to them!"

"But," I said, "surely if you had leisure or inclination to study them all sympathetically, you would end by understanding them."

"I don't think I should. At least I might in a sort of pathological way, as one comes to understand a disease; but I shouldn't understand why they exist. It seems to me, most people aren't fit to exist; and I dare say they have the same opinion about me."

"But are there no people of whose existence you approve?"

"Yes, a few: my friends."

"Surely," cried Ellis, "you flatter us! How often have you said that you don't see why we are this, that, or the other! How often have you complained of our faces, our legs, our arms, in fact, our whole physique, not to mention spiritual blemishes!"

"Well," he replied, "I don't deny that it's a great grief to me to be unable really and objectively to approve of any of my friends. Still——"

"Still," I interrupted, "you have given me the suggestion I wanted. For the relation of affection, however imperfect it may be, gives us at least something which perhaps we shall find comes nearer to what we might conceive to be absolutely Good than anything else we have yet hit upon."

"How so?"

"Well, to begin with, one's friend appears to one, does he not, as an object good in its own nature, not merely by imposition of our own ideal upon an alien stuff, as we said was the case with works of art?"

"I don't know about that!" said Audubon. "In my own case, at any rate, I am sure that my friends never see me at all as I really am, but simply read into me their own ideal. They have just as much imposed upon me their own conception, as if I were the marble out of which they had carved a statue."

"You must allow us to be the judges of that," I replied.

"Well, but," he said, "anyhow you can't deny that such illusions are common. What lover ever saw his mistress as she really is?"

"No," I said, "I don't deny that. But at the same time I should affirm that the truer the love, the less the illusion. In what is commonly called love, no doubt, the physical element is the predominant, or even the only one present; and in that case there may be illusion to an indefinite extent. But the love which is based upon years of common experience, which has grown with the growth of the whole person, in power and intelligence and insight, which has survived countless disappointments and surmounted countless obstacles, the love of husband and wife, the love, as we began by saying, of friends—such love, as Browning says boldly, 'is never blind.' And such love, I suppose you will admit, does exist, however rarely?"

"Yes, I suppose so."

"Well, then, in the case of such a love, it is the object as it really is, not as it has been falsely fashioned by the imagination, that is directly apprehended as good. And you cannot fairly say that its Good is merely the ideal of the lover transferred to the person of the loved."

"But," objected Leslie, "though that may be so, yet still the Good, that is the person, does inhere in an alien stuff—the body."

"But," I replied, "*is* the body alien? Is it not rather an expression of the person? as essential, somehow or other, as the soul?"

"Certainly!" cried Ellis. "Give me the flesh, the flesh!

> 'Not with my soul, Love!—bid no soul like mine
> Lap thee around nor leave the poor sense room!
> Take sense too—let me love entire and whole—
> Not with my soul.'"

"I don't agree with the sentiment of that," said Leslie, "and anyhow, I don't see how it bears on the question. For the point of the poem is rather to emphasize than to deny the opposition between body and soul."

"Yes," replied Ellis, "but also to suggest what you idealists call the transcending of it."

"Do you mean that in the marriage relation, for example . . ."

"Yes, I mean that in that act the flesh, so to speak, is annihilated at the very moment of its assertion, and what you get is a feeling of total union with the person, body and soul at once, or rather, neither one nor the other, but simply that which is in and through both."

"I should have thought," objected Leslie, "it was rather a case of the soul being merged in the body."

"That depends," replied Ellis.

"Yes," I said, "it depends on many things! But what I was thinking of was that, quite apart from that experience, and in the moments of sober observation, one does feel, does one not, a correspondence between body and soul, as though the one were the expression of the other?"

"I don't know," objected Audubon. "What I feel is much more often a discrepancy."

"But still," I urged, "even when there appears to be a discrepancy to begin with, don't you think that in the course of years the spirit does tend to stamp its own likeness on the flesh, and especially on the features of the face?"

"'For soul is form,'" quoted Leslie, "'and doth the body make.'"

"Yes," I said, "and that verse, I believe, is not merely a beautiful fancy of the poet's, but rather as the Greeks maintained—and on such a point they were good judges—a profound and significant truth. At any rate, I find it to be so in the case of the people I care about—though there I know Audubon will dissent. In them, every change of expression, every tone of voice, every gesture has its significance; there is nothing that is not expressive—not a curl of the hair, not a lift of the eyebrows, not a trick of speech or gait. The body becomes, as it were, transparent and pervious to the soul; and that inexplicable element of sense, which baffles us everywhere else, seems here at last to receive its explanation in presenting itself as the perfect medium of spirit."

"If you come to that," cried Ellis, "you might as well extend your remarks to the clothes. For they, to a lover's eyes, are often as expressive and adorable as the body itself."

"Well," I said, "the clothes, too, are a sort of image of the soul, 'an imitation of an imitation,' as Plato would say. But, seriously, don't you agree with me that there is something in the view which regards the body as the 'word made flesh,' a direct expression of the person, not a mere stuff in which he inheres?"

"Yes," he said, "there may be something in it. At any rate, I understand what you mean."

"And in so far as that is so," I continued, "the body, though it be a thing of sense, would nevertheless be directly intelligible in the same way as the the soul?"

"Perhaps, in a sort of way."

"And so we should have in the person loved an object which, though presented to sense, would be at once good and intelligible; and our activity in relation to this object, the activity, that is, of love, would come nearer than any other experience of ours to what we might call a perfect Good?"

"But," objected Leslie, "it is still far enough from being the Good itself. For after all, say what you may about the body being the medium of the soul, it is still body, still sense, and, like other sensible things, subject to change and decay, and in the end to death. And with the fate of the body, so far as we know, that of the person is involved. So that this, too, like all other Goods of sense, is precarious."

"Perhaps it is," I said, "I cannot tell. But all that I mean to maintain at present is that in the activity of love, as we have analysed it, we have something which gives us, if it be only for a moment, yet still in a real experience, an idea, at least, a suggestion, to say no more, of what we might mean by a perfect Good, even though we could not say that it be the Good itself."

"But what, then, would you call the Good itself?"

"A love, I suppose, which in the first place would be eternal, and in the second all-comprehensive. For there is another defect in love, as we know it, to which you did not refer, namely, that it is a relation only to one or two individuals, while outside and beyond it proceeds the main current of our lives, involving innumerable relations of a very different kind from this."

"Yes," cried Ellis, "and that is why this gospel of love, with all its attractiveness, which I admit, seems to me, nevertheless, so trivial and absurd. Just consider! Here is the great round world with all that in it is, infinite in time, infinite in space, infinite in complexity; here is the whole range of human relations, to say nothing of those that are not human, of activities innumerable in and upon nature and man himself, of inventions, discoveries, institutions, laws, arts, sciences, religions; and the meaning and purpose and end of all this we calmly assert to be—what? A girl and a boy kissing on the village green!"

"But," I protested, "who said anything about boys and girls and kisses and village greens?"

"Well, I suppose that is love, of a sort?"

"Yes, of a sort, no doubt; but not a very good one."

"You are thinking, then, of a special kind of love?"

"I am thinking of the kind which I conceive to be the best."

"And what is that?"

"One, as I said just now, that should be eternal and all-comprehensive."

"And so, in the end, you have nothing better than an imaginary heaven to land us in!"

"I have no power, I fear, to land you there. But I believe there is that dwelling within you which will not let you rest in anything short."

"Then I fear I shall never rest!"

"That may be. But meantime all I want to do is to ascertain, if we can, the meaning of your unrest. I have no interest in what you call an imaginary heaven, except in so far as its conception is necessary to enable us to interpret the world we know."

"But how should it be necessary? I have never found it so."

"It is necessary, I think, to explain our dissatisfaction. For the Goods we actually realize always point away from themselves to some other Good whose realization perhaps, as you say, for us is impossible. But even if the Good were chimerical, we cannot deny the passion that pursues it; for it is the same passion that urges us to the pursuit of such Goods as we really can attain. And if we want to understand the nature of that passion, we must understand the nature of its Good, whether it be attainable or no. Only it is for the sake of life here that we need that comprehension, not for the sake of life somewhere else."

"But do you reduce our passion for Good to this passion for Love?"

"I don't 'reduce' it; I interpret it so."

"And so we come back to the girl and the boy and the village green!"

"No! we come back to the whole of life, of which that is only an episode. Let me try to explain how the thing presents itself to me."

"By all means! That is what I want."

"Very well; I will do my best. Let us look then at life just as it is. Here we find ourselves involved with one another in the most complex relations—economic, political, social, domestic, and the rest; and about and in these relations centres the interest of our life, whether it be pleasurable or painful, empty or full, or whatever its character. Among these relations some few perhaps—or, it may be, even none—realize for a longer or shorter time, with more or less completeness, that ultimate identity in diversity, that 'me in thee' which we call love; the rest comprise various degrees of attraction and repulsion, hatred, contempt, indifference, toleration, respect, sympathy, and so on; and all together, always changing, dissolving, and combining anew, weave about us, as they cross and intertwine, the shifting, restless web we call life. Now these relations are an effect and result of the pursuit of Good; but they are never the final goal of that pursuit. The goal, I think, would be a perfect union of all with all; and is not attained by anything that falls short of this, whether the defect be in depth or in extent. And that is how it is that love itself, even in its richer phases, and still more in those which are merely light and sensual, though, as I think, through it alone can we form our truest conception of Good, yet, as we have it, never is the Good, even if it appear to be so for the moment; for those who seek Good, I believe, will never feel that they have found it merely in union with one other person. For what love gains in intension it is apt to lose in extension; so that in practice it may even come to frustrate the very end it seeks, limiting instead of expanding, narrowing just in proportion as it deepens, and, by causing the disruption of all other ties, impoverishing the natures it should have enriched. Or don't you think that this happens sometimes, for instance in married life?"

"I do indeed."

"And, on the other hand," I continued, "it may very well be that one who passes through life without attaining the fruition of love, yet with his gaze always set upon it, in and through many other connections, may yet come closer to the end of his seeking than one who, having known love, has sunk to rest in it then and there, as though he had come already to his journey's end, when really he has only reached an inn upon the road. So that I am far from thinking, as you pretended to suppose, that the boy and girl on the village green realize then and there the consummation of the world."

"Still," he objected, "I do not see, in the scheme you put forward, what place is left for the common business of life—for the things which really do, for the most part, occupy and possess men's minds, and the more, in my opinion, the greater their force and capacity."

"You mean, I suppose, war and politics, and such things as that?"

"Yes, and generally all that one calls business."

"Well," I said, "what these things mean to those who pursue them, I am not as competent as you to say. But surely, what they are in essence is just, like most other activities, relations between human beings—relations of command and obedience, of respect, admiration, antagonism, comradeship, infinitely complex, infinitely various, but still all of them strung, as it were, upon a single thread of passion; all of them at tension to become something else; all pointing to the consummation which it is the nature of that which created them to seek, and all, in that sense, paradoxical as it may sound, only means to love."

"You don't repudiate such activities then?"

"How should I? I repudiate nothing. I am not trying to judge, but, if I could, to explain. It is the men of action, I suppose, who have the greatest extension of life, and sometimes, no doubt, the greatest intension too. But every man has to live his own way, according to his opportunities and capacity. Only, as I think myself, all are involved in the same scheme, and all are driven to the same consummation."

"A consummation in the clouds!"

"I do not know about that; but at any rate, and this is the important point, that which urges us to it is here and now. Everything is rooted in it. Our pleasures and pains alike, our longing and dissatisfaction, our restlessness never-to-be-quenched, our counting as nothing what has been attained in the pressing on to more, our lying down and rising up, our stumbling and recovering, whether we fail, as we call it, or succeed, whether we act or suffer, whether we hate or love, all that we are, all that we hope to be springs from the passion for Good, and points, if we are right in our analysis, to love as its end."

Upon this Audubon broke out:—"That's all very well! But the one crucial point you persistently evade. It may be quite true, for aught I know, that the Good you describe is the Good we seek—though I am not aware of seeking it myself. But, after all, the real question is, Can we get it? If not, we are mere fools to seek it."

"So," I said, "you have brought me to bay at last! And, since you challenge me, I am bound to admit that I don't know whether we can get it or no."

"Well then," he said, impatiently, "what is the good of all this discussion?"

"Clearly," I replied, "no good at all, if there be no Good, which is the point to which you are always harking back. But you have surely forgotten the basis of our whole argument?"

"What basis?"

"Why, that from the very beginning we have been trying to find out, not so much what we know (for on that point I admit that we know little enough), as what it is necessary for us to believe, if we are to find significance in life."

"But how can we believe what we don't know?"

"Why," I replied, "we can surely adopt postulates, as indeed we always do in practical life. Every man who is about to undertake anything makes the assumption, in the first place, that it is worth doing, and in the second place that it is possible to be done. He may be wrong in both these assumptions, but without them he could not move a step. And so with regard to the business of life, as a whole, it is necessary to assume, if we are to make anything of it at all, both that there is Good, and that we know something about it; and also, I think, that it is somehow or other realizable; but I do not know that any of these assumptions could be proved."

"But what right have we, then, to make such assumptions?"

"We have none at all, so far as knowledge is concerned. Indeed, to my mind, it is necessary, if we are to be honest with ourselves, that we should never forget that they are assumptions, so long as they have not received definite proof. But still they are, I think, as I said, assumptions we are bound to make, if we are to give any meaning to life. We might perhaps call them 'postulates of the will'; and our attitude, when we adopt them, that of faith."

"Faith!" protested Wilson, "that is a dangerous word!"

"It is," I agreed. "Yet I doubt whether we can dispense with it. Only we must remember that to have 'faith' in a proposition is not to affirm that it is true, but to live as we should do if it were. It is, in fact, an attitude of the will, not of the understanding; the attitude of the general going into battle, not of the philosopher in his closet."

"But," he objected, "where we do not know, the proper attitude is suspense of mind."

"In many matters, no doubt," I replied, "but surely not in those with which we are dealing. For we must live or die; and if we are to choose to do either, we must do so by virtue of some assumption about the Good."

"But why should we choose to do either? Why should not we simply wait?"

"But wait how? wait affirming or denying? active or passive? Is it possible to wait without adopting an attitude? Is not waiting itself an attitude, an acting on the assumption that it is good to wait?"

"But, at any rate, it does not involve assumptions as large as those which you are trying to make us accept."

"I am not trying to make you do anything; I am only trying to discover what you make yourself do. And do you, as a matter of fact, really dispute the main conclusions to which we have come, or rather, if you will accept my phrase, the main 'postulates of the will' which we have elicited?"

"What are they? Let me have them again."

"Well," I said, "here they are. First, that Good has some meaning."

"Agreed!"

"Second, that we know something about that meaning."

"Doubtful!" said Dennis. "But it will be no use now to resume that controversy."

"No," I replied, "only I thought I had shown that if we know nothing about it, then, for us, it has no meaning; and so our first assumption is also destroyed, and with it all significance in life."

"Well," he said, "go on. We can't go over all that again."

"Third," I continued, "that among our experiences the one which comes nearest to Good is that which we called love."

"Possible!" said Dennis, "but a very tentative approximation."

"Certainly," I agreed, "and subject to constant revision."

"And after that?"

"Well," I said, "now comes the point Audubon raised. Is it necessary to include also the postulate that Good can be realized?"

"But surely," objected Wilson, "here at least there is no room for what you call faith. For whether or no the Good can be realized is a question of knowledge."

"No doubt," I replied, "and so are all questions—if only we could know. But I was assuming that this is one of the things we do not know."

"But," he said, "it is one we are always coming to know. Every year we are learning more and more about the course and destiny of mankind."

"Should you say, then," I asked, "that we are nearer to knowing whether or no the soul is immortal?"

He looked at me in sheer amazement; and then, "What a question!" he cried. "I should say that we have long known that it isn't."

"Then," I said, "if so, we know that the Good cannot be realized."

"What!" he exclaimed. "I had not understood that your conception of the Good involved the idea of personal immortality."

"I am almost afraid it does," I replied, "but I am not quite sure. We have already touched upon the point, if you remember, when we were considering whether we must regard the Good as realizable in ourselves, or only in some generation of people to come. And we thought then that it must somehow be realizable in us."

"But we did not see at the time what that would involve, though I was afraid all along of something of the kind."

"Well," I said, "for fear you should think you have been cheated, we will reconsider the point; and first, if you like, we will suppose that we mean by the Good of some future generation, still retaining for Good the signification we gave to it. The question then of whether or no the Good can be realized, will be the question whether or no it is possible that at some future time all individuals should be knit together in that ultimate relation which we called love."

"But," cried Leslie, "the love was to be eternal! So that *their* souls at least would have to be immortal; and if theirs, why not ours?"

I looked at Wilson; and "Well," I said, "what are we to say?"

"For my part," he replied, "I have nothing to say. I consider the whole idea of immortality illegitimate."

"Yet on that," I said, "hangs the eternal nature of our Good. But may we retain, perhaps, the all-comprehensiveness?"

"How could we!" cried Leslie, "for it is only the individuals who happened to be alive who could be comprehended so long as they were alive."

"Another glory shorn from our Good!" I said. "Still, let us hold fast to what we may! Shall we say that if the Good is to be realized the individuals then alive, so long as they are alive, will be bound together in this relation?"

"You can say that if you like," said Wilson, "and something of that kind I suppose one would envisage as the end. Only I'm not sure that I very well know what you mean by love."

"Alas!" I cried, "is even that to go? Is nothing at all to be left of my poor conception?"

"You can say if you like," he replied, "and I suppose it comes to much the same thing, that all individuals will be related in a perfectly harmonious way."

"In other words," cried Ellis, "that you will have a society perfectly definite, heterogeneous, and co-ordinate! 'There's glory for you!' as Humpty Dumpty said."

"Well," I said, "this is something very different from what we defined to be Good! But this, at any rate, you think, on grounds of positive science, that it might be possible to realize?"

"Yes," replied Wilson; "or if not that, I think at any rate that science may ultimately be in a position to decide whether or no it can be realized."

"But," I said, "do you not think the same about personal immortality?"

"To be honest," he replied, "I do not think that the question of personal immortality is one which science ought even to entertain."

"But," I urged, "I thought science was beginning to entertain it. Does not the 'Society for Psychical Research' deal with such questions?"

"'The Society for Psychical Research!'" he exclaimed. "I do not call that science."

"Well," I said, "at any rate there are men of a scientific turn of mind connected with it." And I mentioned the names of one or two, whereupon Wilson broke out into indignation, declaring with much vehemence that the gentlemen in question were bringing discredit both upon themselves and the University to which they belonged; and then followed a discussion upon the proper objects and methods of science, which I do not exactly recall. Only I remember that Wilson took up a position which led Ellis, with some justice as I thought, to declare that science appeared to be developing all the vices of theology without any of its virtues—the dogmatism, the "index expurgatorius," and the whole machinery for suppressing speculation, without any of the capacity to impose upon the conscience a clear and well-defined scheme of life. This debate, however, was carried on in a tone too polemic to elicit any really fruitful result; and as soon as I was able I endeavoured to steer the conversation back into the smoother waters from which it had been driven.

"Let us admit," I said, "if you like, for the sake of argument, that on the question of the immortality of the soul we do not and cannot know anything at all."

"But," objected Wilson, "I maintain that we do know that there is no foundation at all for the idea. It is a mere reflection of our hopes and fears, or of those of our ancestors."

"But," I said, "even if it be, that does not prove that it is not true; it merely shows that we have no sufficient reason for thinking it to be true."

"Well," he said, "put it so, if you like; that is enough to relegate the notion to the limbo of centaurs and chimaeras. What we have no reason to suppose to be true, we have no reason to concern ourselves with."

"Pardon me," I replied, "but I think we have, if the idea is one that interests us, as is the case with what we are discussing. We may not know whether or no it is true, but we cannot help profoundly caring."

"Well," he said, "I may be peculiarly constituted, but, honestly, I do not myself care in the least."

"But," I said, "perhaps you ought to, if you care about the Good; and that is really the question I want to come back to. What is the minimum we must believe if we are to make life significant? Is it sufficient to believe in what you call the 'progress of the race'? Or must we also believe in the progress of the individual, involving, as it does, personal immortality?"

"Well," said Wilson, "I don't profess to take lofty views of life—that I leave to the philosophers. But I must say it seems to me to be a finer thing to work for a future in which one knows one will not participate oneself than for one in which one's personal happiness is involved. I have always sympathized with Comte, pedant as he was, in the remark he made when he was dying."

"Which one?" interrupted Ellis. "'Quelle perte irréparable?' That always struck me as the most humorous thing ever said."

"No," said Wilson, gravely, "but when he said that the prospect of death would be to him infinitely less sublime, if it did not involve his own extinction; the notion being, I suppose, that death is the triumphant affirmation of the supremacy of the race over the individual. And that, I think myself, is the sound and healthy and manly view."

"My dear Wilson," cried Ellis, "you talk of lofty views; but this is a pinnacle of loftiness to which I, for one, could never aspire. Positively, to rejoice in the extinction of the individual with his faculties undeveloped, his opportunities unrealized, his ambitions unfulfilled—why it's sublime! its Kiplingese—there's no other word for it! Shake hands, Wilson! you're a hero."

"Really," said Wilson, rather impatiently, "I see nothing strained or high-faluting in the view. And as to what you say about faculties undeveloped and the rest, that seems to me unreal and exaggerated! Most men have a good enough time, and get pretty much what they deserve. A healthy, normal man is ready to die—he has done what he had it in him to do, and passed on his work to the next generation."

"I have often wondered," said Ellis, meditatively, "what 'normal' means. Does it mean one in a million, should you say? Or perhaps that is too large a proportion? Some people say, do they not, that there never was a normal man?"

"By 'normal,'" retorted Wilson, doggedly, "I mean average, and I include every one except a few decadents and faddists."

At this point, seeing that we were threatened with another digression, I thought it best to intervene again.

"We are diverging," I said, "a little from the issue. Wilson's position, as I understand him, is that the prospect of the future Good of the race is sufficient to give significance to the life of the individual, even though he realize no Good for himself."

"No," replied Wilson, "I don't say that; for I think he always does realize sufficient Good for himself."

"But is it because of that Good which he realizes for himself that his life has significance? Or because of the future Good of the race?"

"I don't know; both, I suppose."

"You do not think then that the future Good of the race is sufficient, by itself, to give significance to the lives of individuals who are never to partake in it?"

"I don't like that way of putting the question. What I believe is, that in realizing his own Good a man is also contributing to that of the race.

There is no such antagonism between the two ends as you seem to suggest."

"I don't say that there is an antagonism; but I do insist that there is a distinction. And I cannot help feeling—and this is where we seem to disagree—that in estimating the Good of individual lives we must have regard to that which they realize in and for themselves, not merely to that which they may be contributing to produce some day in somebody else."

"These 'somebody elses,'" cried Ellis, "being after all nothing but other individuals like themselves! so that you get an infinite series of people doing Good to one another, and none of them getting any Good for themselves, like the islanders who lived by taking in one another's washing!"

"Well, but," said Wilson, "supposing I consent, for the sake of argument, to let you estimate the worth of life by the Good which individuals realize in themselves. What follows then?"

"Why, then," I said, "it would, I think, be very hard to maintain that we do most of us realize Good enough to make it seem worth while to have lived at all, if indeed we are simply extinguished at death. At any rate, if we set aside an exceptional few, and look frankly at the mass of men and women, judging them not as means to something else, but as ends in themselves, with reference not to happiness, or content, or acquiescence, or indifference, but simply to Good—if we look at them so, can we honestly say that there is enough significance in their lives to justify the labour and expense of producing and maintaining them?"

"I don't know," he replied, "they probably think themselves that there is."

"Probably," I rejoined, "they do not think about it at all. But what I should like to know is, what do you think?"

"I don't see," he objected, "how I can have any opinion; the problem is too vast and indeterminate."

"Is it?" cried Audubon, intervening in his curious abrupt way, and with more than his usual energy of protest. "Well, indeterminate or no, it's the one point on which I have no doubt. Most people are only fit to have their necks broken, and it would be the kindest thing for them if some one would do it."

"Well," I said, "at any rate that is a vigorous opinion. Does anyone else share it?"

"I do," said Leslie, "on the whole. Most men, if they are not actually bad, are at best indifferent—'sacs merely, floating with open mouths for food to slip in.'"

"Upon my word!" cried Bartlett, "it's wonderful how much you know about them, considering how very little you've seen of them!"

"Oh!" I said, turning to him, "then you do not agree with this estimate?"

"I!" he said. "Oh, no! I am not a superior person! Most men, I suppose, are as good as we are, and probably a great deal better!"

"They might well be that," I replied, "without being particularly good. But perhaps, as you seem to suggest, it might be better to confine ourselves to our own experience and consider whether for ourselves, so far as we can see, we should think life much worth having, supposing death to be the end of it all."

"Oh, as to that, of course I should, for my part," cried Ellis, "and so, I hope, should we all. In fact, I consider it rather monstrous to ask the question at all."

"My dear Ellis," I protested, "you are really the most inconsistent of men! Not a minute ago you were laughing at Wilson for his acquiescence in the extinction of the individual 'with his opportunities unrealized, his faculties undeveloped,' and all the rest of it. And now you appear to be adopting precisely the same attitude yourself."

"I can't help it," he replied; "consistent or no, life's good enough for me. And so it should be for you, you ungrateful ruffian!"

"I am not so sure," I said, "that it should be; not so sure as I was a few years ago."

"Why, you Methuselah, what has age got to do with it?"

"Just this," I replied, "that up to a certain time of life all the Good that we get we take to be prophetic of more Good to come. What we actually realize we value less for itself than for something else which it promises. The moments of good experience we expand till they fill all infinity; the intervening tracts of indifferent or bad we simply forget or ignore. Life is good, we say, because the universe is good; and this goodness we expect to grasp in its entirety, not to-day, perhaps, nor to-morrow, but at least the day after. And so, like the proverbial ass, we are lured on by a wisp of hay. But being, at bottom, intelligent brutes, we begin, in time, to reflect; we put back our ears, and plant our feet stiff and rigid where we stand, and refuse to budge an inch till we have some further information as to the meaning of the journey into which we are being enticed. That, at least, is the point that has been reached by this ass who is now addressing you. I want to know something more about that bundle of hay; and that is why I am interested in the question of personal immortality."

"Which means—to drop the metaphor——?"

"Which means, that I have come to realize that I am not likely to get more Good out of life than I have already had, and that I may very likely get less; or if more in some respects, then less in others. For, in the first place, the world, as it seems, is just as much bad as good, and whether Good or Bad predominate I cannot say. And in the second place, even of what Good there is—and I do not under-estimate its worth—it is but an infinitesimal portion that I am capable of realizing, so limited am I by temperament and circumstance, so bound by the errors and illusions of the past, so hampered by the disabilities crowding in from the future. For though, as I think, the older I get the more clearly I recognize what is good, and the more I learn to value and to perceive it, yet at the same time the less do I become capable of making it my own, and must in the nature of things become less and less so, in so far at least as Goods other than those of the intellect are concerned. And this is a position which seems to be involved in the mere fact of age and death frankly seen from the naturalistic point of view; and so it has always been felt and expressed from the time of the Greeks onwards, and not least effectively, perhaps, by Browning in his 'Cleon'—you remember the passage:

"'. . . . . Every day my sense of joy
Grows more acute, my soul (intensified
By power and insight) more enlarged, more keen;
While every day my hairs fall more and more,
My hand shakes, and the heavy years increase—
The horror quickening still from year to year,
The consummation coming past escape,
When I shall know most, and yet least enjoy—
When all my works wherein I prove my worth,
Being present still to mock me in men's mouths,
Alive still in the phrase of such as thou,
I, I the feeling, thinking, acting man,
The man who loved his life so over-much,
Shall sleep in my urn.'

You see the point; indeed, it is so familiar, I have laboured it, perhaps, too much. But the result seems to be, that while it is natural enough that in youth, for those who are capable of Good, life should seem to be pre-eminently worth the having, yet the last judgment of age, for those who believe that death is the end, will be a doubt, and perhaps more than a doubt, even in the case of those most favoured by fortune, whether after all a life has been worth the trouble of living which has unfolded such infinite promise only to bury it fruitless in the grave."

"I think that's rather a morbid view!" said Parry.

"I do not know," I said, "whether it is morbid, nor do I very much care; the question is, whether it is reasonable, and whether it is not the position naturally and perhaps inevitably adopted not by the worst but by the best men among those who have abandoned the belief in personal immortality."

"That," interposed Wilson, "is surely not the case. One knows of people who, though they have no belief in survival after death, yet maintain a perfectly cheerful and healthy attitude towards life. Harriet Martineau is one that occurs to me. To her, you may remember, life appeared not less but more worth living when she had become convinced of her own annihilation at death; and she awaited with perfect equanimity and calm its imminent approach, not as a deliverance from a condition which was daily becoming more intolerable, but as a fitting crown and consummation to a career of untiring and fruitful activity."

"That," exclaimed Parry with enthusiasm, "is what I call magnanimous!"

"I don't!" retorted Leslie, "I call it simply stupid and unimaginative."

"Call it what you like," said Wilson; "anyhow it is a position which can be and has been adopted."

"Yes," I agreed, "but one which, I think, a clearer analysis of the facts, a franker survey and a more penetrating insight, would make it increasingly difficult to sustain. And after all, an estimate which is to endure must be not only magnanimous but reasonable."

"But to her, and to others like her, it did and does appear to be reasonable. And you ought to admit, I think, that there are cases in which life is well worth living quite apart from the hypothesis of personal immortality."

"I am ready to admit," I replied, "that there are people to whom it seems to be so, but I doubt whether they are very numerous, among those, I mean, who have reflected on the subject, and whose opinions alone we need consider. I, at any rate, have commonly found in talking to people about death—supposing, which is unusual, that they are willing to talk about it at all—that they adopt one of two views, either of which presupposes the worthlessness of life, if life, as we know it, be indeed all."

"What views do you mean?"

"Why, either they believe that death means annihilation, and rejoice in the prospect as a deliverance from an intolerable evil; or they hold that there is a life beyond, and that they will find there the reason and justification for existence which they have never been able to discover here."

"You forget, surely," said Wilson, "a third point of view, which I should have thought was as common as either of the others,—that of those who believe in a life after death, but look forward to it with inexpressible fear of the possible evils which it may contain."

"True," I said, "but such fear, I suppose, is a reflex of actual experience, and implies, does it not, a vivid sense of the evils of existence as we know it? So that these people, too, I should maintain, have not really found life satisfactory, or they would look forward with hope rather than fear to the possibility of its continuance."

"But in their case, at any rate, the hypothesis of personal immortality is an aggravation, not a remedy, of the evil."

"No doubt; but I have been assuming throughout that the hypothesis involves the realization of that Good which, without it, we recognize to be unattainable; and it is only in that sense, and from that point of view, that I have introduced it."

"Well," he persisted, "considering how improbable the hypothesis is, I should be very loth to admit that it is one which it is practically necessary to adopt. And I still maintain that most people do not require it—ordinary simple people, I mean, who do their work and make no fuss about it."

"Perhaps not," I replied, "for it is characteristic of such people to make no hypothesis at all, but to adopt for the moment any view suggested by the state of their spirits. But I believe that if ever you can get a man, no matter how plain and unsophisticated, to reflect fairly upon his own experience, and to look impartially at the facts all round, abstracting from all bias of habit and mood and prejudice, he will admit that if it be true that the individual is extinguished at death, together with all his possibilities of realizing Good, then life cannot rationally be judged to be worth the living, however imperatively we may be compelled to continue to live it."

"But it is just that imperative compulsion," cried Parry, "on which I rely! That seems to me the justification of life—the fact that we are forced to live! I trust that instinct more than all the ratiocination in the world!"

"But," I said, "when you say that you trust the instinct, do you mean that you judge it to be good?"

"Yes, I suppose so."

"Then in trusting the instinct you are really trusting your reason, which judges the instinct to be good, or, if not your reason, the faculty, whatever it be, which judges of Good. And the only difference between us is, that I try to ascertain what we do really believe to be good, whereas you accept and cling to a particular judgment about Good, without any attempt to test it and harmonize it with others."

"But you admit yourself that all your results are tentative and problematical in the extreme."

"Certainly."

"And yet these results you venture to set in opposition to a simple, profound, imperative cry of Nature!"

"Why should I not? For I have no right to suppose that nature is good, except in so far as I can reasonably judge her to be so."

"That seems to me a sort of blasphemy."

"I am afraid," I said, "if I must choose, I would rather blaspheme Nature than Reason. But I hope I am not blaspheming either. For it may be that what you call Nature has provided for the realization of Good. That, at any rate, is the hypothesis I was suggesting; and it is you who appear to be setting it aside."

"But," objected Wilson, "you talk of this hypothesis as if it were something one could really entertain! To me it is not a hypothesis at all; it's simply an inconceivability."

"Do you mean that it is self-contradictory?"

"No, not exactly that. Simply that it is unimaginable."

"Oh!" I said; "but what one can imagine depends on the quality of one's imagination! To me, for example, the immortality of the soul does not seem any harder to imagine than birth and life, and death and consciousness. It's all such a mystery together, if once one begins trying to realize it."

"No one," interposed Ellis, "has put that point better than Walt Whitman."

"True," I replied, "and that reminds me that I think you hardly did justice to his view when you were quoting him a little while ago. It is true that he does, as you said, accept all facts, good and bad, and even appears at times to obliterate the distinction between them. But also, whether consistently or no, he regards them all as phases of a process, good only because of what they promise to be. So that his view really requires a belief in immortality to justify it; and to him such belief is as natural and simple as to Wilson it is absurd. There is a passage somewhere, I remember—perhaps you can quote it—it begins, "Is it wonderful that I should be immortal?"

"Yes," he said, "I remember":

"Is it wonderful that I should be immortal? as every one is immortal;

"I know it is wonderful—but my eyesight is equally wonderful, and how I was conceived in my mother's womb is equally wonderful,

"And passed from a babe, in the creeping trance of a couple of summers and winters to articulate and walk. All this is equally wonderful.

"And that my soul embraces you this hour, and we affect each other without ever seeing each other, and never perhaps to see each other, is every bit as wonderful.

"And that I can think such thoughts as these is just as wonderful,

"And that I can remind you, and you think them and know them to be true, is just as wonderful.

"And that the moon spins round the earth, and on with the earth, is equally wonderful,

"And that they balance themselves with the sun and stars is equally wonderful."

"That," I said, "is the passage I meant, and it shows that Whitman, at any rate, did not share Wilson's feeling that the immortality of the soul is unimaginable."

"Well," said Wilson, "imaginable or no, we have no reason to believe it to be true."

"No reason, indeed," I agreed, "so far as demonstration is concerned, though equally, as I think, no reason to deny it. But the point I raised was, whether, if we are to take a positive view of life and hold that it somehow has a good significance, we are not bound to adopt this, hypothesis of immortality—to believe, that is, that, somehow or other, there awaits us a state of being in which all souls shall be bound together in that harmonious and perfect relation of which we have a type and foretaste in what we call love. For, if it be true that perfect Good does involve some such relation, and yet that it is one unattainable under the conditions of our present life, then we must say either that such Good is unattainable—and in that case why should we idly pursue it?—or that we believe we shall attain it under some other conditions of existence. And according as we adopt one or the other position—so it seems to me—our attitude towards life will be one of affirmation or of negation."

"But," he objected, "even if you were right in your conception of Good, and even if it be true that Good in its perfection is unattainable, yet we might still choose to get at least what Good we can—and some Good you admit we can get—and might find in that pursuit a sufficient justification for life."

"We might, indeed," I admitted, "but also we might very well find, that the Good we can attain is so small, and the Evil so immensely preponderant, that we ought to labour rather to bring to an end an existence so pitiful than to perpetuate it indefinitely in the persons of our luckless descendants."

"That, thank heaven," said Parry, "is not the view which is taken by the Western world."

"The West," I replied, "has not yet learned to reflect. Its activity is the slave of instinct, blind and irresponsible."

"Yes," he assented eagerly, "and that is its saving grace! This instinct, which you call blind, is health and sanity and vigour."

"I know," I said, "that you think so, and so does Mr. Kipling, and all the train of violent and bloody bards who follow the camp of the modern army of progress. I have no quarrel with you or with them; you may very well be right in your somewhat savage worship of activity. I am only trying to ascertain the conditions of your being right, and I seem to find it in personal immortality."

"No," he persisted. "We are right without condition, right absolutely and beyond all argument. Pursue Good is the one ultimate law; whether or no it can be attained is a minor matter; and if to inquire into the conditions of its attainment is only to weaken us in the pursuit, then I say the inquiry is wrong, and ought to be discouraged."

"Well," I said, "I will not dispute with you further. Whether you are right or wrong I cannot but admire your strenuous belief in Good and in our obligation to pursue it. And that, after all, was my main point. On the other question about what Good is and whether it is attainable, I could hardly wish to make converts, so conscious am I that I have infinitely more to learn than to teach. Only, that there is really something to learn, of that I am profoundly convinced. Perhaps even Audubon will agree with me there?"

"I don't know that I do," he replied, "and anyhow it doesn't seem to me to make much difference. Whatever we may think about Good, that doesn't affect the nature of Reality—and Reality, I believe, is bad!"

"Ah, Reality!" I rejoined, "but what is Reality? Is it just what we see and touch and handle?"

"Yes, I suppose so."

"That is a sober view, and one which I have constantly tried to impress upon myself. Sometimes, even, I think I have succeeded, under the combined stress of logic and experience. But there comes an unguarded moment, some evening in summer, like this, when I am walking, perhaps, alone in a solitary wood, or in a meadow beside a quiet stream; and suddenly all my work is undone, and I am overwhelmed by a direct apprehension, or what seems at least for the moment to be such, that everything I hear and see and touch is mere illusion after all, and behind it lies the true Reality, if only I could find the way to seize it. It is due, I suppose, to some native and ineradicable strain of mysticism; or perhaps, as I sometimes think, to the memory of a strange experience which I once underwent and have never been able to forget."

"What was that?"

"It will not be very easy, I fear, to describe, but perhaps it may be worth while to make the attempt, for it bears, more or less, on the subject of our conversation. Once then, you must know, and once only, a good many years ago now, I was put under the influence of anæsthetics; and during the time I was unconscious, or rather, conscious in a new way, I had a very curious dream, if dream it were, which has never ceased to affect my thoughts and my life. It was as follows:

"As soon as I lost consciousness of the world without, my soul, I thought, which seemed at first to be diffused throughout my body, began to draw itself upward, beginning at the feet. It passed through the veins of the legs and belly to the heart, which was beating like a thousand drums, and thence by the aorta and the carotids to the brain, whence it emerged by the fissures of the skull into the outer air. No sooner was it free (though still attached, as I felt with some uneasiness, by a thin elastic cord to the pia mater) than it gathered itself together (into what form I could not say), and with incredible speed shot upwards, till it reached what seemed to be the floor of heaven. Through this it passed, I know not how, and found itself all at once in a new world.

"What this world was like I must now endeavour to explain, difficult though it be to find suitable language; for the things here, of which our words are symbols, are themselves only symbols of the things there. The feeling I had, however, (for I was now identified with my soul, and had forgotten all about my body)—the feeling I had was that of sitting alone beside a river. What kind of country it was I can hardly describe, for there was nowhere any definite colour or form, only a suggestion, such as I have seen in drawings, of vast infinite tracts of empty space. I could not even say there was light or darkness, for my organ of perception did not seem to be the eye; only I was aware of an emotional effect similar to that of twilight, cold, grey, and formless as night itself. The silence was absolute, if indeed silence it were, for it was not by the ear that I perceived either sound or its absence; but something there was, analogous to silence in its effect. And in the midst of the silence and the twilight (since so I must call them) flowed the river, or what seemed such, distinguishable, as I thought at first, rather by the fact that it flowed, than by any peculiarity of substance, colour, or form, from the stretches of empty space that formed its banks. But presently, as I looked more closely, I saw, rising from its surface, dipping, rising, and dipping again, in a regular rhythm, without change or pause, what I can only compare to a shoal of flying fish. Not that they looked like fish, or indeed like anything I had ever seen, but that was the image suggested by their motion. As soon as I saw them I knew what they were: they were souls; and the river down which they passed was the river of Time; and their dipping in and out again was the sequence of their lives and deaths.

"All this did not surprise me at all. Rather, I felt it was something I had always known, yet something inexpressibly flat and disillusioning. 'Of course!' I said to myself, or thought, or whatever may have been my mode of cognition—'Of course! That is it, and that is all! Souls are indeed immortal—why should we ever have imagined otherwise? They are immortal, and what of it? I see the death-side now as I saw the life-side then; and one has as little meaning as the other. As it has been, so it will be, now, henceforth, and for ever, in and out, in and out, without pause or stint, futile, trivial, silly, stale, tedious, monotonous, and vain!' The long pre-occupation of men with religion, philosophy, and art, seemed to me now as incomprehensible as it was ridiculous. There was nothing after all to be interested about! There was simply this! The dreariness of my mood was indescribable, and corresponded so closely to the scene before me that I found myself wondering which was effect, which cause. The silence, the tracts of unformed space, the unsubstantial river, the ceaseless vibration along its surface of infinite moving points, all this was a reflex of my thoughts and they of it. My misery was intolerable; to escape became my only object; and with this in view I rose and began to move, I knew not whither, along the silent shore.

"As I went, I presently became aware of what looked like high towers standing along the margin of the stream. I say they looked like towers, but I should rather have said they symbolized them; for they had no specific shape, round or square, nor any definite substance or dimensions. They suggested rather, if I may say so, the idea of verticality; and otherwise were as blank and void of form or colour as everything else in this strange land. I made my way towards them along the bank; and when I had come close under the first, I saw that there was a door in it, and written over the door, in a language I cannot now recall, but which then I knew that I had always known, an inscription whose sense was:

'*I am the Eye; come into me and see.*'

Miserable as I was, it was impossible that I should hesitate; I did not know, it is true, what might await me within, but it could not be worse and might well be better than my present plight. The door was open; I stepped in; and no sooner had I crossed the threshold than I was aware of an experience more extraordinary and delightful than it had ever been my lot to encounter. I had the sensation of seeing light for the first time! For hitherto, as I have tried to explain, though it has been necessary to speak in terms of sight, I have done so only by a metaphor, and it was not really by vision that I became acquainted with the scene I have described. But now I saw, and saw pure light! And yet not only saw, but, as I thought apprehended it with the other senses, both with those we know and with others of which we have not yet dreamt. I heard light, I tasted and touched it, it enveloped and embraced me; I swam in it as in an element, wafted and washed and luxuriantly lapped. Pure light, and nothing else! No objects, at first! It was only by degrees, and as the first intoxication subsided, that I began to be aware of anything but the medium itself. I saw then that I was standing at what seemed to be a window, looking out over the scene I had just left. But how changed it was! The river now, like a blue and golden snake, ran through a sunny champaign bright with flowers; above it hung a cloudless summer sky; and the happy souls went leaping in and out like dolphins on a calm day in the Mediterranean. On all this I gazed with inexpressible delight; but as I looked an extraordinary thing occurred. The flowery plain before me seemed to globe itself into a sphere; the blue river clasped it like a girdle; for a moment it hung before me like a star, then opened out and split into a thousand more, and these again into others and yet others, till a whole heaven of stars was revolving about me in the most wonderful dance-measure you can conceive, infinitely complex, but never for a moment confused, for the stars were of various colours, more beautiful far than any of ours, and by these, as they crossed and intertwined in exquisite harmonies, the threads of the intricate figure were kept distinct.

"What I was looking upon, I knew, was the same heaven that our astronomers describe; only I was privileged actually to perceive the movements they can only infer and predict. For here on earth our faculties are proportioned to our needs, and our apprehension of time and change is measured by units too small for us to be able to embrace by sense the large and spacious circuits of the stars. But I, in my then condition, had powers commensurate with all existence; so that not only could I follow with the eye the coils of that celestial morrice, but in each one of the whirling orbs, as they approached or receded in the dance, I could trace, so far as I was minded, the course of its secular history; whole series of changes and transformations such as we laboriously infer, from fossils and rocks and hard unmalleable things, being there (as though petrifaction were reversed and solidest things made fluid) unrolled before me, molten and glowing and swift, in a stream of torrential evolution whose moments were centuries. Wonderful it was, and strange, to see the first trembling film creep like a mantle over a globe of fire, shiver, and break, and form again, and gradually harden and cohere, now crushed into ridges and pits, now extended into plains, and tossing the hissing seas from bed to bed, as the levels of the viscous surface rose and fell. Wonderful, too, when the crust was formed and life became possible, how everywhere, in wet or dry, hot or cold alike, wherever footing could be found, came up and flourished and decayed things that root and things that move, winged or finned or legged, creeping, flying, running, breeding, in mud or sand, in jungle, forest, and marsh, pursuing and pursued, devouring and devoured, pairing, contending, killing, things huge beyond belief, mammoth and icthyosaurus, things minute and numerous past the power of calculation, coming and going as they could find space, species succeeding to species, and crowding every point and vantage for life on the heaving tumultuous bosom of eddying worlds.

"Wonderful it was, but terrible, too; for what struck me with a kind of chill, even while I was wrapt in admiration, was the fact that though everything was in constant change, and in the change there was clearly an order and routine, yet I could not detect anything that seemed like purpose. Direction there was, but not direction to an end; for the end was no better than the beginning, it was only different; the idea of Good, in short, did not apply. And this fact, which was striking enough in the case of the phenomena I have described, made itself felt with even more insistence when I turned to consider the course of human history. For that too I saw unrolled before me, not only on our own, but on innumerable other worlds, in various phases and in various forms, both those which we know, and others of which we have no conception, and which I am now quite unable to recall. Men I saw housing in caves, or on piles in swamps and lakes, dwellers in wagons and tents, hunters, or shepherds under the stars, men of the mountain, men of the plain, of the river-valley and the coast, nomad tribes, village tribes, cities, kingdoms, empires, wars and peace, politics, laws, manners, arts and sciences. Yet in all this, so far as I could observe, although, through all vacillations, there appeared to be a steady trend in a definite direction, there was nothing to indicate what we call purpose. Men, I saw, had ideas about Good, but these ideas of theirs, though they were part of the efficient causes of events, were in no sense the explanation of the process. There was no explanation, for there was no final cause, no purpose, end, or justification at all. Man, like nature, was the plaything of a blind fate. The idea of Good had no application.

"The horror I felt as this truth (for so I thought it) was borne in upon me was proportioned to my previous delight. I had now but one desire, to escape, even though it were only back to what I had left. And as the Angel-Boys in 'Faust' cry out to Pater Seraphicus for release, when they can no longer bear the sights they see through his eyes, so I, in my anguish, cried, 'Let me out! Let me out!' And instantly I found myself standing again at the foot of the tower, in that land of twilight, silence, and infinite space, with the souls going down the river, in and out, in and out, futile, trivial, tedious, monotonous, and vain. Looking up, I saw written over the door from which I had emerged, and which was opposite to that by which I had entered, words whose sense was:

'*Eye hath not seen.*'

I walked round the Tower, and found a third door facing the river; and over that was written:

'*Turris scientiae.*'

But all these doors were now closed; nor indeed, had they been open, should I have felt any inclination to renew the experience from which I had escaped. I therefore turned away sadly enough and made my way along the bank towards the second tower.

"Over the door of this was written in the same language as before:

'I am the Ear; come into me and hear.'

The door was open, and I went in, this time with some apprehension, but with still more curiosity and hope. No sooner was I within than I was overwhelmed by an experience analogous to that which had greeted me in the Tower of Sight, but even more ravishingly sweet. This time what I felt was the sensation of pure sound: sound, not merely heard, but, as before in the case of light, apprehended at once by every avenue of sense, and folding and sustaining, as it seemed, my whole being in a clear and buoyant element of tone. It was only by degrees that out of this absolute essence of sheer sound distinctions of rhythm and pitch began to appear, and to assume definite musical form. The theme at first was pastoral and sweet, suggestive of rustling grasses and murmuring reeds, interwoven with which was an exquisite lilting tune, the song of the souls as they sped down the river. But one by one other elements crept into the strain; it increased in volume and variety of tone, in complexity of rhythm and tune, till it grew at length into a symphony so august, so solemn, and so profound, that there is nothing I know of in our music here to which I can fitly compare it. It reminded me, however, of Wagner more than of any other composer, in the richness of its colour, the insistence and force of its rhythms, its fragments of ineffable melody, and above all, its endless chromatic sequences, for ever suggesting but never actually reaching the full close which I knew not whether most to dread or to desire. The music itself was wonderful enough; but more wonderful still was my clear perception, while I listened, that what was being presented to me now through the medium of sound was precisely the same world which I had seen from the Tower of Sight. Every phenomenon, and sequence of phenomena, which I had witnessed there, I recognized now, in appropriate musical form. The foundation of all was a great basal rhythm, given out on something that throbbed like drums, terrible in its persistence and yet beautiful too; and this, I knew, represented the mechanical basis of the world, the processes which science knows as 'laws of motion' and the like, but which really, as I then perceived, might more aptly be described as the more inveterate of Nature's habits. Upon this foundation, which varied, indeed, but by almost imperceptible gradations, was built up an infinitely complex structure of intermediate parts, increasing from below upwards in freedom, ease and beauty of form, till high above all floated on the ear snatches of melody, haunting, poignant, meltingly tender, or, as it might be, martial and gay exquisite in themselves, yet never complete, fragments rather, as it seemed, of some theme yet to come, which they had hardly time to suggest before they were torn, as it were, from their roots and sent drifting down the stream, to reappear in new settings, richer combinations, and fairer forms; and these, I knew, were symbols of the lives and deaths of conscious beings.

"As this character of the music and its representative meaning grew gradually clearer to me, there began to mingle with my delight a certain feeling of anguish. For while, on the one hand, I passionately desired to hear given out in full the theme which as yet had been only suggested in fragmentary hints, on the other, I knew that with its appearance the music would come to a close, just at the moment when its cessation would involve the keenest revulsion of feeling. And this moment, I felt, was rapidly approaching. The rhythm grew more and more rapid, the instruments scaled higher and higher, the tension of chromatic progressions was strained to what seemed breaking point, till suddenly, with an effect as though a stream, long pent in a gorge, had escaped with a burst into broad sunny meadows, the whole symphony broke away into the major key, and high and clear, chanted, as it seemed, on ten thousand trumpets, silver, æthereal, and exquisitely sweet for all their resonant clangour, I heard the ultimate melody of things. For a moment only; for, as I had foreseen, with the emergence of that air, the music came abruptly to a close; and I found myself sitting bathed in tears at the door of the tower on the opposite side to that by which I had entered; and there once more was the land of silence, twilight, and infinite space, with the souls going down the river, in and out, in and out, futile, trivial, tedious, monotonous and vain!

"As soon as I had recovered myself, I looked up and saw written over the door the inscription :

'Ear hath not heard.'

And going round to the side facing the river, I saw there inscribed :

'Turris Artis.'

"Whereupon, full of perplexity, I made my way down towards the third tower, reflecting, as I went, in a curious passion at once of hope and fear, 'Neither this, then, nor that, neither Eye nor Ear, has given me what I sought. Each is a symbol ; but this, as it seems, a more perfect symbol than that ; for it, at least, is Beauty, and the other was only Power. But is there, then, nothing but symbols? Or shall I, in one of these towers, shall I perhaps find the thing that is symbolized?'

"By this time I had reached the third tower, and over the door facing me I saw written :

'I am the Heart ; come into me and feel.'

I entered without hesitation, and this time I was met by an experience even stranger and more delightful than before, but also, I fear, more indescribable. At first, I was aware of nothing but a pure feeling, which was not of any particular sense, (as, before, of sight and hearing,) but was rather, I think, the general feeling of Life itself, the kind of diffused sensation of well-being one has in health, underlying all particular activities. In this sensation I seemed, as before, to be lapped, as in an element ; but this time the feeling did not pass. On the contrary, I found, when I came to myself, that I actually was in the river, leaping along with the other souls in such an ecstasy of physical delight as I have never felt before or since. Such, at least, was my first impression ; but gradually it changed into something which I despair of rendering in words, for indeed I can hardly render it in my own thoughts. Conceive, however, that as, according to the teaching of science, every part of matter is affected by every other, insomuch that, as they say, the fall of an apple disturbs the balance of the universe ; so, in my experience then, (and this, I believe, is really true) all souls were intimately connected by spiritual ties. Nothing that happened in one but was somehow or other, more or less obscurely, reflected in the rest, so that all were so closely involved and embraced in a network of fine relations that they formed what may be compared to a planetary system, sustained in their various orbits by force of attraction and repulsion, distinguished into greater and lesser constellations, and fulfilling in due proportion their periods and paths under the control of spiritual laws. Of this system I was myself a member ; about me were grouped some of my dearest friends ; and beyond and around stretched away, like infinite points of light, in a clear heaven of passion, the world of souls. I speak, of course, in a figure, for what I am describing in terms of space, I apprehended through the medium of feeling ; and by 'feeling' I mean all degrees of affection, from extreme of love to extreme of hate.

For hate there was, as well as love, the one representing repulsion, the other attraction; and by their joint influence the whole system was sustained. It was not, however, in equilibrium; at least, not in stable equilibrium. There was a trend, as I soon became aware, towards a centre. The energy of love was constantly striving to annihilate distance and unite in a single sphere the scattered units that were only kept apart by the energy of hate. This effort I felt proceeding in every particular group, and, more faintly, from one group to another: I felt it with an intensity at once of pain and of rapture, such as I cannot now even imagine, much less describe; and most of all did I feel it within the limits of my own group, of which some of those now present were members. But within this group in particular I was aware of an extraordinary resistance. One of its members, I thought, (I mention no names,) steadily refused either to form a closer union with the rest of us, or to enter into more intimate relations with other groups. This resistance I felt in the form of an indescribable tension, a tension which grew more and more acute, till suddenly the whole system seemed to collapse, and I found myself in darkness and alone, being dragged down, down, by the cord which attached me to my body. At the same time there was a roaring in my ears, and I saw my body, as I thought, like a fearful wild beast with open jaws; it swallowed me down, and I awoke with a shock to find myself in the operator's room, with a voice in my ears which somehow sounded like Audubon's, though I afterwards ascertained it was really that of the assistant, uttering the rather ridiculous words, 'I don't see why!'

"That, then, was the end of my dream, and I have never since been able to continue it, and to discover what was written over the other doors of the third tower, or what lay within the towers I did not enter. So that I have had to go on ever since with the knowledge I then acquired, that whatever Reality may ultimately be, it is in the life of the affections, with all its confused tangle of loves and hates, attractions, repulsions, and, worst of all, indifferences, it is in this intricate commerce of souls that we may come nearest to apprehending what perhaps we shall never wholly apprehend, but the quest of which alone, as I believe, gives any significance to life, and makes it a thing which a wise and brave man will be able to persuade himself it is right to endure."

With that I ended; and Wilson was just beginning to explain to me that my dream had no real significance, but was just a confused reproduction of what I must have been thinking about before I took the æther, when we were interrupted by the arrival of tea. In the confusion that ensued Audubon came over to me and said: "It was curious your dreaming that about me, for it is exactly the way I should behave."

"Of course it is," I replied, "and that, no doubt, is why I dreamt it."

"Well," he said, "you can say what you like, but I really do *not* see why!" And with that the conversation I had to report closed.